SCIENCE AND ENGINEERING POLICY SERIES

General Editors Sir Harrie Massey
Sir Frederick Dainton

Science and Policy

The International Stimulus

ALEXANDER KING, C.B.E., D.SC.

OXFORD UNIVERSITY PRESS 1974

Oxford University Press   *Ely House, London, W.1*

Glasgow	Delhi
New York	Bombay
Toronto	Calcutta
Melbourne	Madras
Wellington	Karachi
Cape Town	Lahore
Ibadan	Dacca
Nairobi	Kuala Lumpur
Dar es Salaam	Singapore
Lusaka	Hong Kong
Addis Ababa	Tokyo

CASEBOUND ISBN 0 19 858310 9

OXFORD UNIVERSITY PRESS 1974

Typesetting by
Linocomp Ltd., Marcham, Berkshire

Printed in Great Britain by
Fletcher & Son Ltd, Norwich
and bound by
Richard Clay (The Chaucer Press) Ltd, Bungay, Suffolk

Contents

Introduction

'Science policy' is a term which has come into use comparatively recently, and although in Great Britain the Advisory Council for Scientific Policy had been set up in 1947 under the Lord President of the Council, the concept of creating separate and coherent policies concerning the national organization of science and the allocation of resources to research was hardly known elsewhere. Indeed, when the first Conference of Ministers of Science took place in Paris in 1963, only three of the twenty-two Member countries of the Organization for Economic Cooperation and Development (OECD) had Ministers of or for science, although in one case it was a special responsibility under the Prime Minister. The other countries were mainly represented by Ministers of Education, indicating that less than ten years ago science was regarded by most governments as a branch of cultural policy, although many government departments possessed applied research units or financed research by contract.

The last ten years have seen a mushrooming of interest in science policy which has accompanied the rapid growth of resources for research and development—ministers of science, science policy councils, and the like have appeared in most of the industrialized nations and in many of the less developed countries also. Science and technology have become too influential in the growth of the economy and society and demand too high a proportion of national resources to be left to expand without some policy framework. Moreover, the subject, which is inherently complex, has attracted considerable academic attention. There are several important science policy units in

Introduction

both British and other European universities, while in the United States they can be counted in their tens.

This rapid growth, both of scientific research and of its institutions and policies, has flourished under a mystique. It had been somewhat naïvely assumed, mainly as a consequence of the overwhelming importance of science in the Second World War, that more research and development would automatically lead to greater prosperity, better health of the people, more security from enemies (or power to attack them), and enhanced national prestige, and this has induced parliamentarians everywhere to vote vast sums of money to fields and projects about which they know next to nothing. The research scientists themselves have not been slow to exploit this mystique to provide the resources which their specialized enthusiasms required.

Of course, research has had enormous success during recent decades and its contributions through the technology built upon it have transformed the world: radio, television, and rapid methods of transportation have shrunk space and made the interdependence of nations a demonstrated reality. Vast new science-based industries have provided prosperity and utterly changed the pattern of world trade. An important fraction of mankind has moved from subsistence to affluence. Life is longer and less degraded by disease. But all this has changed the nature of society, has led to the population explosion, the concentration of people in cities, and has fundamentally altered the nature of work and its satisfactions to the extent that an increasing number of people are questioning the values of contemporary society and are feeling instinctively that the quality of life is leaking away. Furthermore, unforeseen and unwanted side-effects of the very technology which has freed us from want, for example, through environmental pollution, are leading many people, and especially the young, to question the values of society and of the technology on which it has been built. Technology has become a dirty word in some quarters and science itself is suspect, its mystique shattered, despite the fact that new knowledge and hence new research will be urgently required to tackle the cluster of intertwining problems to which the applications of science have given rise.

This abrupt change in public opinion, already beginning to be reflected in the policies of various governments, obviously calls for a reassessment, not only of the goals of society, but of the research policies and priorities for their attainment. An important step in this direction was taken when the Ministers of Science of the OECD countries, meeting in Paris in October 1971, not only accepted the need for change but agreed unanimously on the main thrusts to be expected from scientific activities in the 1970s. Whether this was mere lip-service or a convinced acceptance of the need for a basic reorientation of science policy remains to be seen.

In the report of the high-level group of independent scientists appointed by the Secretary-General of OECD under the chairmanship of Dean Harvey Brooks of Harvard University to advise on new concepts of science policy, such policy is defined as 'a deliberate and coherent basis for national decisions influencing the investment, institutional structures, creativity and utilisation of scientific research'. The report admits that no country has, as yet, succeeded in introducing such a comprehensive approach, although many are striving in that direction. Other and newer definitions equate science policy with the mastery of technological progress, a much wider concept which places the subject clearly within a social framework.

The topic is approached in different ways in different countries. Inclusion in the Brooks Report (1971) definition of 'application' implicitly brings technology within the concept of science policy and, despite the very different criteria for success which apply to disinterested fundamental research at one extreme and technological development at the other, there is much sense in considering the two together in view of their inter-relations. In some instances, national science policy concentrates mainly on the problems of allocating funds for basic research, in others great emphasis is placed on technology; in most national structures for science policy consideration defence R and D is excluded.

When comparing national science policies and structures, a further confusion arises from different understandings as to what is included in the term 'science'. The research councils and other national agencies for science in most countries of the world equate science with knowledge—*la science, Wissenschaft, nauk*—and the grant-giving bodies in these countries are responsible for the support, for example, of historical and literary research, as well as for chemistry and physics; academies of science have in general equally wide concern with the whole spectrum of learning. In the English-speaking world, on the other hand, 'science' tends to be restricted to the natural sciences and science policy to such sciences and the technology based on them, although of recent years the social sciences have begun to be included, if somewhat marginally.

This Anglo-Saxon heresy which restricts the meaning of science is probably at the origin of the condition known as the 'two cultures' although the mystique of science with its esoteric and mathematical vocabularies accentuates the divergence. The wider conceptual context of science to Latin, Russian, Japanese, and other minds is probably the reason why Margaret Mead can say that what the two cultures fear is a preoccupation of a small elite of the Anglo-Saxon world, of little significance elsewhere.

Since, however, the situation which has necessitated the creation of national science policies, and especially those of resource allocation, has arisen from the mushrooming of resources for R and D, mainly in the physical sciences and their technologies, the problems are the same in all industrialized countries, unrelated to the philosophical assumptions.

The new turn of events, which stresses the complex, multivariant nature of contemporary problems and the need for multidisciplinary means to attack them, is already beginning to change the attitude of the 'Anglo-Saxons' to the conceptual framework of science. For example, the agreed necessity of assessing in advance the social and even cultural consequences of new technologies can hardly be restricted to the physicist or the engineer. This trend may well go far in re-establishing an understanding of the unity of all knowledge which the rapid growth and ultra-specialization of the natural sciences have obscured.

In the early 1960s the question was raised as to why any policy for science was required: should not funds be distributed entirely on the basis of the promise of research and the established reputations of the research leaders? The idea of policy connoted a bureaucratization of science and a *dirigisme* which might inhibit creativity. In fact, at an earlier stage the relatively moderate resources devoted to research were mainly used either within the mission-orientated laboratories and agencies of government itself, or else distributed through the 'judgement of peers principle' to projects within universities and institutes for fundamental research with the cultural aims of extending knowledge and enriching higher education. With the rising costs and extent of R and D which came mainly as a result of scientific prestige carried over from the war and a dawning appreciation on the part of governments that research was useful and, in fact, a necessary national investment, competition for resources began to become important—not only between scientists hoping for support of their own research ideas but also between the various departments of governments.

Resources were growing rapidly, it is true, but in nearly all countries they were considerably less than demands for research support. Where the opportunity for promising investment in research is much greater than the resources available, choice has to be made, priorities established, and policies evolved. The very concept of priorities in research was at first anathema to the scientists but it soon became clear, for example, in radio-astronomy as in other 'big' sciences, that each professor of astronomy could not be given equipment costing as much as a radiotelescope and, indeed, smaller countries could not afford a single example of such equipment. National co-operative schemes as well as international cost-sharing solutions began to appear, and it was clear that in most cases governments knew better than to attempt interference in the substance and detail of research and restricted themselves to allocation between broad fields and negotiations on particularly expensive projects. The research community, riding securely on the bandwagon of rapidly growing research budgets, co-operated well on the whole, although occasionally with some bitterness.

The last two decades have, however, been the period of euphoria for science, which with its mystique has been something of a *chasse gardée*. Decisions were made with the minimum of conflict, eased by a situation of continuous expansion. The profound changes now taking place in the established relationship between supply and demand, between governments, parliaments, science, and the public, between economic, social, and cultural objectives face science policy with much more difficult decision-making and painful transitions, especially if there is to be a levelling-off in resources. As the Brooks Report pointed out, 'even basic science will have to respond to needs for selective emphasis, determined by the social, political, and industrial environment'.

Science is, of course, like other intellectual activities, inherently international in its nature and methods. As research becomes more sophisticated, autonomous discovery by the single great mind becomes more rare. Each new research is a step of advance taken on the basis of contributions to the subject from many parts of the world and finding its extension and application often in distant places by quite different teams of scientists. It is not surprising that international co-operation in research has developed vigorously, if not always successfully. In Europe in particular, with its fractionation into a large number of small political entities, such co-operation has appeared to offer a partial solution to resource shortage, especially where 'big science' is concerned. This development has met many difficulties, particularly in relating international activity to national programmes. There is, in fact, no international or European science policy as yet within which these problems can find a rational solution. Nevertheless, the discussion of research co-operation internationally and of science policy has given rise to much serious exchange of experience and formulation of criteria which, as we shall see, has greatly influenced national developments in this new and quickly changing area of policy. Experience shows that international exchange of experience is particularly effective between countries facing similar problems, as yet uncertain of the solutions and as yet lacking entrenched institutions. It is much easier for countries as for individuals to profit from the successes and failures of others when they have not yet finally chosen their own directions.

In this book we shall deal mainly with this rapid accumulation and confrontation of experience between a group of countries, marked by a high level of industrialization and mainly operating a market economy. The specifically British problems will be dealt with in detail in other publications of the same series, but the common problems raised should throw light on what is a continuing debate in our own as in other countries.

1

Prelude to policy: science and government before 1947

The history proper of an idea begins when it is adequately formulated and has a conscious and separate existence in the minds of men. This stage has barely been reached with regard to the concept of science policy, which, as a phrase, is variously understood. In some circles and in some countries, the existence or necessity for such a policy is still contested; in others it is said to be an old fact rather than a new concept. Even amongst the practitioners of science policy, some define it in somewhat narrow terms of allocation and management of the resources which government provides for research, while others conceive it very broadly in terms of ensuring that new knowledge is generated and applied to the development of society in its entirety. The concept is continually evolving and modifying: some would even regard it as an essentially temporary, if important, phenomenon.

Since, however, the term 'science policy' is in common, if imprecise use, we shall take as the period of its formal arising the years between 1947 and 1955, which saw the creation in most of the scientifically advanced countries of national research organizations, policy or co-ordination groups, and the appointment of ministers specifically designated to guide a nation's scientific effort as a whole, in the best interests of the community.

In this chapter we shall describe the experience of a few countries in their pre-science-policy attempts to organize research activities towards the achievement of national objectives, to create national laboratories, and to secure the application of the results of research.

Science and national life: some early associations

One of the earliest significant attempts to relate science and national effort was the creation of the Royal Society of London by

1

King Charles II in 1662 to encourage 'the improvement of natural knowledge'. The Society, in which the King took great personal interest, was concerned with the development of learning and also with its application. It was conceived in apolitical terms and its royal charter required its Fellows to pledge not to meddle in 'moralls or poleticks'. The early Fellows of this now exclusively 'scientific' society were by no means restricted to experimentalists but, as Bishop Spratt in his contemporaneous *History of the Royal Society* (1667) testifies, its membership was to draw upon 'all the professions', as well as on independent savants—'gentlemen free and unconfined'. It included poets such as Dryden and Cowley, men of letters such as Evelyn and Pepys (who was a professional civil servant), architects, including Wren, as well as scientists such as Boyle and Newton, in addition to philosophers and theologians. This was an interesting moment in history. A European monarch of lively mind, eager to incorporate in his thinking the best of available knowledge, combined the concept of the 'well-rounded ideals of renaissance humanism' in close association with the new experimentalism within an organization which would encourage learning and provide advice at the national level. The advisory function of the Royal Society persists, although its advice is no longer exclusively sought or always forcefully given.

The early Fellows of the Royal Society were eminently respectable conformists, in fact the first scientific 'establishment', but they possessed a new zeal for inquiry. Bishop Spratt praised the rational and practical objective of the Society 'to increase the powers of all mankind and to free him from the bondage of errors'. There is a recognition here, not only of the power of knowledge to free men from superstition, but also of the possibility that through the application of new discovery man could 'enrich himself with all the benefits of fruitfulness and plenty'—a primitive expression from a royalist and conventional society which would not be out of place in the rationalist and socialist societies of today. Although the Royal Society was deeply concerned with elaborating natural philosophy in the broadest sense and with applying it in agriculture, industry, and navigation, a century was to pass before a substantial realization of these aims could be achieved, through the accumulation of knowledge and acceleration of discovery which culminated in the industrial revolution.

A new wave of interest in the interaction of science and practical affairs came at the end of the eighteenth century. The phlogiston theory was dead and the atomic concept of matter was replacing it; the chemical elements were being discovered and mechanical invention flourished. It was not surprising, therefore, that men of inquiring mind should have a renewed vision of a world in which there would be an understanding of nature and of humanity and also that universal prosperity might be generated through exploitation of knowledge. In England, such possibilities brought together a group of outstanding individuals whose intellectual curiosity and entrepreneurial energy was to ignite the fuse that exploded the industrial revolution upon Europe. These men—scientists, philosophers, and the new type of industrialists—assembled for dissussion, debate, speculation, and self-criticism in an independent, formless, and short-lived society to which they gave the curious name of the 'Lunar Society'. This was an allusion to the fact that it was their custom to meet over dinner at the house of one of their members, often in Birmingham at the home of Joseph Priestly, on nights when the moon was full. (Replete with speculation and well wined and dined, they could then drive safely home in their carriages to various places in the Midlands.) The significance of these meetings was tremendous. Through the society, inventors such as James Watt and industrialists such as Wedgwood and Boulton were intimately concerned with the development of the new scientific theories and the emergence of the industrial arts. Learning and application were conceived as evolving together, and the impact of the new thinking on society, religion, the nature of man, and of the universe was freely discussed by individuals well aware that they were witnessing and indeed consciously assisting in the birth of a new world.

While the industrial achievements of the members of this club were quickly felt through the creation of a new industrial society— for they were in fact the fathers of the industrial revolution— industry developed through empirical invention rather than by the application of scientific discovery. It took more than a century for subjects such as chemistry and physics to develop their substance to the extent of dominating innovation and industrial growth as we know it today, and it is sad to think that in the brutal development of British and European industry in the eighteenth century the universal vision, social awareness, and philosophical basis which the Lunar Society had given to industry at the outset was so completely lost. The Lunar Society had, of course, no official links; it is doubtful if the government of the time was even aware of its existence. As a group it was as nonconformist as the Royal Society had been traditional, and its political outlook was liberal, to say the least: it had great sympathy with the French and American revolutions (and, indeed, Priestly's house was burnt to the ground by a mob incited by respectable citizens outraged by a club dinner to celebrate the fall of the Bastille).

Early American scientific thought was similarly based: Baconian, rational, and revolutionary. The fact of the American revolution made this inevitable. The new government had to destroy the remnants of dynastic power, build immediately a republican system based on the individual citizen as the unit of political power, and create new institutions of government policy through rational and experimental processes. The American revolution was intellectual and social as well as political; its leaders, liberal and practical men, were forced to become innovators in more than political institutions. Washington, a rich landowner, was a surveyor and engineer with a flair for scientific education; Franklin, a physicist and inventor (when since have we seen a top-level scientist in the role of ambassador?); Jefferson, an intellectual of broad scientific attainment who stimulated a wide range of experimental studies; John Adams, who succeeded Washington, was convinced that applied science could provide the basis of American development; Alexander Hamilton used fiscal and tariff incentive to encourage industrial development and subsidized research and invention. In the early days of the new republic, more attention was given to the application of science rather than to the creation of new knowledge. Thus, much activity was devoted to mapping the country, surveying its resources, agricultural improvement, and providing statistical and census services. Thus there was an intuitive policy for the use of science which was reflected in the resources provided for investigations, but this was still a long way from becoming a policy for science.

Science institutions before 1947

The U.S.A.: striving for order in complexity

The vast size of the United States, with the need to open up new terrains, exploit agricultural possibilities and mineral resources, as well as to create an advanced industrial society, called for the

organization and use of science and technology to an extent unknown elsewhere during the last century and now paralleled only
in the Soviet Union. From the beginning, the growth of American
scientific agencies took place side by side with that of private enterprise industries. For many years the stress was on applied rather
than on fundamental research. Even after the Second World War
Vannevar Bush (1945), in his report to President Roosevelt entitled
Science, the endless frontier, was pleading for the building-up of
fundamental research in the United States from which application
would come spontaneously, the implicit assumption being that even
at so recent a date America was relying for its technological
development too much on European basic science.

For more than a century, therefore, the United States has been
building institutions to stimulate and co-ordinate research and its
application. The size and richness of the country is such that
diversity and even replication of scientific institutions are an inherent feature of American tradition and of its particular type of
government, that pluralistic approaches and even duplication of
effort are valuable and provide a 'fertile disorder' which the country
can well afford.

It is particularly in times of war that governments give serious
attention to scientific advice and build up their research institutions.
The history of American scientific institutions has consisted essentially of the creation at (or after) the outbreak of each war of a
new central body with co-ordinating, advisory, and research-
funding functions. At the next crisis, the earlier institution has been
found too weak, academic, or inbred to meet the new demands, and
so a new body has been created, while the older ones persist and
coexist. The first of this series of organizations was the Smithsonian
Institution, which derived from a bequest made by a disgruntled
English chemist, James Smithson, hardly known in the U.S.A., who
died in 1839. This institution, established in 1846, had its museum
to house national collections. Its first secretary, Joseph Henry, was
a professional physicist who put emphasis on research and the
publication of its results, and was probably the first scientist to
envisage widespread support of research by the award of free
grants and the sponsoring of clearly formulated research projects.
The Smithsonian, which is still an important national institution,
is a strange organization. Its board includes the President, Vice-
President, Chief Justice, and Cabinet of the country. This may well

5

be the only function of the President's Cabinet vested in law. In practice it is run by a board of regents which delegates executive responsibility to a secretary which it appoints. Although bound to the government by law, the Smithsonian is largely autonomous: it has now little influence on government science, having become essentially the administration of a series of museums and a zoo, but it has had considerable influence in the stimulation and creation of other more active scientific institutions.

A critical point in the evolution of American science policy was the outbreak of the Civil War. This was a time when railroads, the steamship and the telegraph had appeared, while artillery had developed sufficiently to alter the position of attack and defence, and hydrogen-filled balloons were used for observation. The need for scientific advice for the war was recognized and a temporary 'permanent commission' of three scientists was formed to examine new inventions. The commission, despite the lack of budget and staff and the possibility of systematic work, operated well and, after a long and bitter argument, the National Academy of Sciences was founded by law. It had the function of acting as a scientific advisory body to all the agencies of government caring to put their problems to it. Initially, a series of committees of inquiry were set up to deal with subjects such as coinage, weights and measures, prevention of the corrosion of ships' bottoms, magnetic deviation of the compass in iron ships, and the investigation of hydrometers to measure the alcohol content of liquor for revenue purposes. The results of these activities on war were modest enough. A second function of the Academy was to provide honours for its members and, since it was a self-perpetuating group, this became its dominant feature and has remained so until recently. It has, however, contributed greatly to the quality of American research.

The years following the Civil War saw an expansion of the government's scientific effort, mainly through bureaux attached to the various executive departments. In this way a series of important scientific institutions came into being, such as the National Bureau of Standards, the Geological Survey, the Weather Bureau, the Bureau of Mines, and the National Advisory Committee for Aeronautics. On various occasions commissions were set up with a view to establishing co-ordinating machinery between them or even to the establishment of a Department of Science—but nothing came of it. Important progress was made in agriculture through a series of federal research programmes, while the 'land-grant colleges' were established in every state to provide training in agriculture and the mechanical arts, to undertake research, and to operate extension services. This system, originally criticized harshly by the academics on grounds of quality, succeeded well in spreading the scientific method throughout agriculture and in many other fields throughout the country.

When the First World War broke out, the old problem of scientific advice to government came once more to the fore. The National Academy still had the formal possibility of providing counsel, but its limited membership and lack of connection with government on practical affairs prevented it from being exploited. However, on the proposal of the Academy, a National Research Council was established as an appendage. The NRC was broadly based and able to include on its committee members of the Academy and also engineers and industrial technologists. Its wartime performance was effective mainly through the wisdom and energy of its research director, Robert A. Milliken. It was never adequately financed, however, most of its funds coming from the Carnegie and Rockefeller Foundations. It did nevertheless function as a central scientific agency and clearing-house for scientific information and personnel. Its only effective means of obtaining government research funds was to commission its scientists in appropriate units of the army and navy. As the war proceeded, its programmes fell more and more under military control and depended increasingly on proposals formulated by the armed services for research, rather than on the ideas generated by its members. This was a period of enormous upsurge of industrial development, and the NRC had an important role in stimulating the necessary technologies; in so doing, forged a permanent link between American science and industry.

These contacts were maintained throughout the inter-war years, and the NRC acquired a competence in the funding of research and the award of fellowships. Since, however, it had to rely mainly on private sources of finance, it was unable to become a forceful central organization for American science. On the books it still ranked as an agency of government, but in practice it lost official contact.

The depression of the 1930s and the New Deal stressed for the first time the economic and social relationship of natural science and technology. Again attempts were made to evolve a coherent policy by the creation of a Science Advisory Board, but once again, as with the Academy and the NRC, government interest did not reach the point of providing a budget. Endless discussions took place on 'the great social objectives of science', but that was all. When the Second World War broke out, then, no adequate central scientific organization existed, nor any means for giving coherent scientific advice to the government, despite the efforts of generations of scientists to provide for such functions. It was obvious from the outset, however, that the war might well be lost or won on technological supremacy and that structures and mechanisms had to be provided to ensure the development and utilization of scientific and engineering resources on an unprecedented scale. An important impetus was given to this, even before Pearl Harbour, by the arrival in the United States of a British technical mission led by Sir Henry Tizard, which brought with it the famous black box of British war secrets, including microwave radar. A National Defence Research Committee was set up in 1940, which at first sight had many of the features of earlier attempts to organize American science. This body, however, possessed the will, the energy, the resources, the political support, and above all the leadership which its gigantic task necessitated. The majority of projects undertaken by NDRC were initially from lists prepared by the armed forces; it possessed, however, the right of initiative to sponsor new, promising, and often highly speculative developments suggested by recent scientific discovery, and freedom of judgement concerning what to undertake and how to carry it out. In this way ideas emanating from scientific discovery were quickly fed into defence technology; and these, as was soon to appear, were the significant war-winning items. For the first time science was a major innovator in defence rather than a servant of conventional technology and invention.

The NDRC decided not to create laboratories of its own but to have its work done by contract in the most appropriate university and industrial laboratories, without regard to geographic pattern. Even this institution proved to be too narrow, however, and after a year the Office of Scientific Research and Development (OSRD) was created which incorporated both the NDRC and the Medical Research Council, functioning with unimpaired effectiveness within the larger organization. The OSRD, in which research and technology were organically united, ensuring the total mobilization of science for the war, its correlation with military thinking and with engineering development and production. Furthermore, it was established as an executive arm of the government; its director, Vannevar Bush, had full administrative responsibility as well as direct and easy access to President Roosevelt. This enabled Bush to deal on equal terms with military leaders and to push forward ideas in which the latter was disinterested. The OSRD was an immediate and overwhelming success. In wartime circumstances, it provided science policy and performance and enjoyed the total use of American scientific potential. Among other things, it made possible the final scientific achievement of the war—the use of nuclear fission. Bush and his senior colleagues, J. B. Conant and K. J. Compton, never envisaged the OSRD as other than a temporary, wartime organization, but its success projected American science beyond the point of no return as a major national investment on survival and in the future.

In the organization of American science today, the strong centralism of the OSRD has been abandoned. The present pattern is of strong governmental agencies for space, atomic energy, agriculture, health, etc., with the National Science Foundation responsible for supporting fundamental research and graduate education in science. On the central co-ordinating level is the President's Special Assistant for Science, with his Science Policy Committee concerned with the breadth and future of American science as a whole, and the Federal Council for Science and Technology to review the government's own research programmes (see, however, p. 61). On the edge still function the older organizations: the Smithsonian, the National Research Council, and the Academy, which has of recent years developed a new energy. Behind all this is the massive and productive research and development effort of American industry.

Development of scientific organizations in Britain

Fundamental research flourished increasingly in Britain throughout the latter part of the nineteenth century; science, education, and industrial application received an impetus at the time of the Great Exhibition of 1861. It was only towards the end of the century, however, that the government's own research effort became organized, first with the establishment of the Geological Survey and, in 1899, by the creation of the National Physical Laboratory, which, while executively a government laboratory, was under the scientific supervision of a committee set up for the purpose by the Royal

Society. The Lord President of the Council, normally a senior minister without executive responsibility, became the minister responsible for policy on such matters. Later, the political mechanism of the government for science consisted of small groups of interested ministers for industrial, medical, and agricultural research respectively, formally constituted as the committees of the Privy Council. This grafting of a new function on to an old stem never really flourished and, in fact, the committees met infrequently.

It was not until the First World War that a coherent research organization emerged. It was found, soon after hostilities commenced, that British science and industry had depended too much on continental, and especially German, innovation and that a major effort was required to build up scientific structures and ensure that the results of their research were fed into industry. In addition to emergency wartime measures, the Department of Scientific and Industrial Research (DSIR) was therefore set up in 1915. This organization developed consistently until 1965, when a new system replaced it. There was a serious interruption of growth and activity of the DSIR during the Second World War but vigorous development thereafter. Its scope and principles of work, briefly described below, were evident in the newly created organization. The DSIR, nominally a department of state, reported through its permanent secretary to the Lord President of the Council and later to the Minister for Science; corresponding research councils for medical and agricultural research were later created with the same ministerial connection.

Although the DSIR was formally a government organ, its policy and programmes were developed with the help of an advisory and, later, executive committee consisting of academic scientists, industrialists, and trades-union representatives. Equally, the various national laboratories of the Department such as the National Physical Laboratory, the Chemical Research Laboratory, the Road and Building Research Stations, the Geological Survey, the Hydraulics, Fuel, and Forest Products Laboratories were all advised by boards of independent scientists, together with industrialists and, later, trade unionists from the sector in question. A further function was given to the DSIR as early as 1917, namely the creation of research associations for particular industries. These organizations, which at one time amounted to fifty, were financed partly by government, through the DSIR, and partly by subscribing member firms.

This system, which has many interesting aspects, has endeavoured to undertake research of interest to industries as a whole and not to replace the competitive development which is the function of the individual firm. The role of the DSIR was not merely one of passive financing, but of promoting the creation of research associations in co-operation with groups of progressive industrialists from the various industries. Very little strategic guidance was given to the research associations by the Department, which bent over backwards to refrain from influencing their programmes, with the motive of maintaining the reality of their independence from government control. The research association movement, despite its many critics, still functions in the contemporary British system.

The national system of three research councils reporting to a single, senior minister had the appearance of coherence, but the contact between the councils was in fact rather superficial and, apart from the inevitable function of the Treasury, there was no systematic approach to the allocation of resources between needs, not yet seen as competitive. It should be realized also that there was no effective contact with the defence science effort. Despite these weaknesses, the system had many valuable features: it concentrated the civilian research activities of the government within a flexible structure, advised and managed by scientists, that went just about as far as was possible, within a pre-war civil service, to ensure conditions within which scientific creativity could flourish. Its chief lack was probably insufficient contact with day-to-day user needs for research.

Up to the Second World War, the size of the British science system was small enough for internal adjustments and policy direction to be in the hands of a few, outstanding personalities belonging to the same coterie. Coherence and mutual understanding were probably achieved rather effectively, if utterly informally, through frequent, easy, but often unplanned contacts between the leading figures of the Royal Society, the research council secretaries, and senior civil servants, all of whom were habitués of the Athenaeum Club.

Before the war broke out, research priority was, of course, focused on defence needs. The service departments had their own research stations and had programmes which involved many of the outstanding scientists of the country, at least in an advisory capacity. For example, the work of the Aeronautical Research Council and

11

its committees was particularly successful, and their development of microwave radar, the jet engine, and the proximity fuses had a dominant influence on the war. The defence research stations were vastly extended during the war by recruiting scientists from industry, the universities, and the DSIR network. Their work was as usual supervised by committees, many of whose members were independent scientists and came under administrative control of three departments: the Admiralty, the Ministry of Supply, and the Ministry of Aircraft Production. Collectively, they constituted the counterpart of the OSRD in America. In general it functioned well; research was fully articulated with operational needs, and effective use was made of the best scientific brains of the country. Apart from the giants—Sir Henry Tizard and Lord Cherwell, whose incompatability has given rise to much debate—there was Cockcroft at the Ministry of Supply, Blackett and Goodeve at the Admiralty, Bernal and Zuckerman at Combined Operations, and many more. During this period also, the techniques of operational research were elaborated and brilliantly applied. This approach combined statistical method, analysis and clear formulation of problems, and the establishment of a relationship of confidence and easy communication between the scientists and defence chiefs. That this relationship could be created and sustained was one of the surprises of the war and a great source of strength within the British effort.

In comparison with the system in the United States, the British war science system was somewhat diffuse and unco-ordinated, even though British science was totally mobilized and both university and industrial technical skills well employed. By 1942 complaints of lack of a central science strategy were mounting in both political and scientific circles. In an attempt to meet these criticisms, a group of three senior science advisers was appointed within a new co-ordinating ministry, the Ministry of Production. The three advisers, who soon called themselves the three blind mice, despite their easy access to ministers, quickly found that they had no real possibilities of co-ordination. They therefore settled down to tackling emergency problems which did not fall clearly within the three main defence groups; for example, it was from their work that DDT emerged as a major technical factor in the war in the East. Thus the untidy and loose system of defence research continued until the end of the war, a precarious if brilliant example of British 'muddling through'.

During this period, however, much serious discussion began on the basic need for a national science policy. As early as 1941, a committee on Commonwealth co-operation was formed at the Royal Society which, impressed by the success of scientific relations between the constituent countries of the Commonwealth for war, began to make post-war plans, which led to the major British Commonwealth Science Conference of 1947. More important, an eminent but very remote central organ was created during the war in London, a Scientific Advisory Council under the chairmanship of Lord Hankey, who had been the brilliant secretary of the Cabinet during the First World War. This committee included the President of the Royal Society and the secretaries of the three research councils. It had, in reality, no influence on war science but did some useful thinking about post-war needs.

When the war ended, government officials and scientists were equally impressed by the part which research and development had played in winning the war, saw clearly their potentialities for peacetime development, and were determined that a new and permanent partnership between government and science should be constructed in the national interest. Many measures were taken, including the creation of a scientific civil service and the establishment of an Advisory Council for Scientific Policy—and this is where we enter the era of science policy.

Canada: a policy for science but no science policy

History and geography have determined Canada's strivings towards a science policy. A country of vast size, its small population is concentrated in a few areas along the 3000 miles of boundary with the United States. Most of the industries of Canada are associates of American or, to a lesser extent, British firms, depending for new technology on the laboratories of their parent companies. This has necessitated an important governmental role in research stimulation. Between the two world wars a National Research Council was established, initially to build up research in the universities through grants and fellowships. This was a wise policy since it provides year by year a growing body of competent research workers which, despite substantial emigration south of the border where research employment abounded, provided the basis for the Canadian war science effort which was closely related to that of the two other countries which we have discussed. When university research had

13

been soundly established, the NRC then erected its own central laboratories in Ottawa, which have an excellent record of research achievement. During the war, the NRC was strongly involved in research technology, but its work has nevertheless been dominantly fundamental rather than applied research in character. A number of regional research institutions were created in the provinces. At the same time the various government departments generated strong programmes in resource development, particularly related to agriculture, fisheries, and minerals. When the war ended, this situation persisted for nearly two decades with little central concept of policy. NRC has been criticized for its failure to grasp the problems of industrial research. The Canadian NRC is an example of a national scientific institution with broad functions, succeeding unusually well in generating research activities of very high scientific quality but not succeeding in, and indeed until recently hardly attempting, the equally difficult task of ensuring an intimate connection between scientific effort and national needs.

2

Governments and the support of research

In this chapter we shall review briefly the general functions which governments have assumed during the present century. We have seen that the great upsurge of the industrial arts, which have made possible our present material prosperity, flourished initially through invention rather than systematic scientific investigation. However, during the hundred years which elapsed from the beginning of the industrial revolution, the natural sciences, such as chemistry and physics, had accumulated knowledge—for example, understanding of the laws of thermodynamics, of electricity, of synthetic organic chemistry—which made possible the production at a reasonable cost of multitudes of substances unknown in nature and with properties useful to man. By the beginning of this century, therefore, science had much to offer and research held out prospects of much more to come. Industry began to invest in research, and indeed whole new branches such as the dyestuffs and pharmaceutical industries grew directly from discoveries made in the chemical laboratory. Government finance began to be available in modest amounts for research and scientific education, and official organizations had to be created, for example, for geological survey and for the creation and maintenance of standards.

By the end of the first decade of the present century, therefore, several governments were creating and operating their own scientific institutions for special fields of application. This movement was given a new impulse during the 1914–18 War, when it became apparent, for example, that the chemical monopoly of Germany, based on the work of her classical scientists, would have to be emulated elsewhere. The process of transfer of technology had begun.

Soon the governments of all industrialized and developing countries possessed central scientific organizations of some sort which grew, changed, and evolved into the scientific organizations which exist today.

These vary greatly in character from country to country, in accordance with size, level of industrialization, indigenous raw materials, environment, and historical traditions. Some are great and powerful organs of the state, operating networks of national laboratories; others essentially provide stimulus and advice or distribute government money in the form of fellowships, grants to individuals or institutions for research, or contracts to industry for development work. Some were conceived as part of the conventional civil service; others are quasi-independent organizations in receipt of government finance. In some countries learned societies and academies of science exist side by side with official scientific organizations and have the double function of both encouraging fundamental research and presenting scientific papers and also distributing national funds. They may concentrate essentially on basic research or may co-operate with industry in the promotion of applied research and technological development. In some countries the scientific establishment is highly centralized; in others a pluralistic approach is adopted.

In most countries, therefore, the functions of government with regard to research have grown by accretion as needs have been identified and have not been deliberately or systematically planned. They have generally been conceived as service activities or as means of extending knowledge, and it is only recently that scientific research or science in the larger sense have begun to be regarded as agents of national development rather than as support activities.

In spite of the diversity of form exhibited by national scientific institutions the types of research attracting direct government support are remarkably uniform from country to country. It may be useful at this stage to enumerate these briefly.

Science and education

Equality of opportunity for education at all levels is now accepted in most countries, and the costs constitute one of the major national expenditures, exceeding in many countries that of defence. The basic social cultural objectives of education entail the teaching of science as one of the major cultural ingredients of today. Furthermore, the training of skilled manpower is an important goal of the educational system, which means that scientific and technological subjects have great importance, especially at the post-secondary level.

Research in universities

In most countries encouragement of fundamental research is a general government charge for three purposes—the extension of learning, the vitality of teaching at higher levels and the production of professionally skilled manpower for the government's own research needs, for teaching at university level and for industry. Usually the general overheads of research of this type are included in the overall financing of the universities, but often this is topped up by special funds to provide for the needs of research scientists of promise, to allow the acquisition of sophisticated instrumentation or to encourage background (oriented fundamental) research in areas where new basic knowledge is required for applicational purposes. Since the end of the Second World War there has been a tendency in some countries for defence and other ministries to offer contracts to university departments, including some abroad, to undertake particular research projects. Although such topics are generally of a background research nature, only indirectly related to defence objectives and free from security restrictions, it is increasingly felt that too great a proportion of such contract research is inappropriate to university institutions, since however germane it may be to the normal work of a laboratory, acceptance of projects determined from outside inhibits to some extent the natural development of basic research, which depends so much on the free choice of the professor in following the lines of his own inspiration.

In many instances, the distribution of government grants to research workers as well as the financing of special research projects is undertaken by national research councils, which pronounce on the merits of proposals by the system known as 'judgement by peers', i.e. they are examined by panels of experts in the specialist fields in question. This system is obviously sound in general, but it has its limitations, especially in the smaller countries where experts in a particular specialization are few and, although eminent, may have become over-traditional and not always open to new approaches. If young, interested research workers with fresh views are to be supported, even if they have not yet won respectability, alternative sources of financing should be available. There is a role here for the independent foundations.

As the importance of research for national objectives—economic, defence, cultural—became more clearly recognized by governments, special measures were often taken to encourage (but not to dictate) some degree of priority in the national research programmes. It is generally accepted that the university provides the most propitious environment for fundamental research because of the symbiotic relationship between higher instruction and scientific investigation and particularly through the special and creative association between the outstanding research leader and cohorts of young research students. Nevertheless the free system of choice of topic in the universities and their slowness to adapt to new needs and at times to take up new subjects has led governments to supplement the normal university research system by other mechanisms. For example, in France the Centre National de la Recherche Scientifique (CNRS) has established a whole series of institutions of research mainly within the universities but complementary as far as research is concerned to the normal faculty system. In Germany, the Max Planck Gesellschaft has, with government funds, created an important network of fundamental research institutes. In the United Kingdom the Medical and Agricultural Research Councils have for long operated a system of special research units, located within universities but separate from the normal academic structure. In France again the CNRS has provided special and substantial financial means to attract research talent to new subjects, which were felt important for the national good but not yet spontaneously attracting sufficient research effort (*actions concertées*).

Support for research activities requiring expensive equipment

While arrangements of the type described above cater for special research needs, including those which demand expensive installations and highly sophisticated equipment, governments frequently sponsor institutions such as astronomical, radio-astronomical, or meteorological observatories, oceanographic research ships, etc. Although these are concerned with research of a basic nature, they do not easily fit into the university organization. Centres for nuclear research, which demand expensive particle accelerators and other equipment, often fall into this category, since such research with its high cost and often elaborate maintenance needs can unbalance the normal functioning of a university. In order to preserve the academic atmosphere, so propitious for creativity in fundamental research, such institutions are in some cases managed by individual universities or may be organized and operated—as in the Brookhaven Nuclear Laboratory in the United States—by a group of universities. In Japan some of the fields of 'big research' are organized within the university system rather than being operated directly by the government. This is the case with reactor engineering as well as other aspects of nuclear research and also space research. To meet these needs, the Japanese Ministry of Education has organized some fourteen national research institutions as part of the university system and belonging, as it were, to the universities as a whole. Each institute is for administrative convenience managed by a particular university on behalf of the system as a whole. This mechanism, which is not restricted to particularly costly fields of research, has some clear advantages. For example, it enables the maintenance of a first-class and extremely comprehensive institute for solid-state physics, operated by the University of Tokyo, which permits all sub-specializations of this important field to be covered within a single large institution, with obvious advantages of cross-fertilization.

Defence research

Only governments can assume responsibility for the complex military technology of today and the whole range of research and development necessary to sustain it. In the larger countries such research was initially undertaken in establishments of the military departments, but with increasing complexity and scale, recourse is frequently made to develop contracts with industry and to a lesser extent the universities. This is particularly the case in the United States, where the sophistication and advanced technological nature of defence made it necessary to organize in new and flexible ways so as to attract the best scientific and engineering brains. An important ingredient in the success of science during the Second World War was the establishment of a real and continuing dialogue between the leading scientists and the defence chiefs. This made it possible for the military to appreciate the potentialities of new scientific discoveries for strategic objectives and provided the scientists with a practical understanding of military technological requirements. Such a relationship was possible in the emergency condition of the early 1940s, but well-nigh impossible to maintain within the peacetime military establishment with its inevitable inflexibilities. In attempts to solve this problem many institutional innovations have been attempted in the United States, for example in the formation of non-profit-making companies, able to pay the rate for the job and to provide conditions more propitious for creative work than could be found in the normal governmental structures.

The practice of undertaking so much advanced research for military objectives raised considerable controversy in the United States as to whether the sophisticated defence technology made a real contribution to the development of industry generally. Undoubtedly the major developments during the war gave a tremendous impulse to civilian development. One has only to cite atomic power, radar, jet aircraft, computers, television, and even DDT. Subsequent 'spin-off' from military research is less easy to assess. Certainly some advances, including high-temperature alloys, new ceramics, and electronic devices, have had a civilian importance, but the main effect has probably been less direct, through a general increase in the technological level and in the management of complex systems. Some of the non-profit-making organizations just mentioned, such as the RAND Corporation, have contributed significantly to the development of a systems approach to a wide range of civilian problems.

Research for public utilities

Since, in the modern state, government activity is so extensive, it requires, as in other sectors of the economy, scientific research and technological development in fields where the government has direct applicational interest. Examples are road research, both with regard to the construction of highways, road safety, and traffic control; forestry; maintenance of the environment, including the provision of clean water and air; geological survey; fire prevention; the establishment of pure food and drug standards; loose-bed hydraulics in relation to rivers and docks and coastal maintenance. In many countries, great national laboratories deal with such topics, although other such work is done either in semi-autonomous institutions, such as the TNO Organization in the Netherlands, or by contract with industry and the universities.

Research of a general character

Most governments support a considerable volume of research as a background service for the economy on topics which the individual enterprise could not be expected to deal with. Examples are the establishment and maintenance of standards of weight, electricity, and radioactivity; provision of reference materials, such as especially pure chemicals; and in some cases basic work on metallurgical and meteorological subjects and on corrosion.

Research for small unit-size industries

There are some important economic sectors, such as agriculture and building constructions, where the unit enterprise—the farm or the small building contractor—is too small to undertake its own research and where, even if it could do so, duplication would be excessive. Consequently all governments support extensive agricultural research and some maintain building research stations, laboratories concerned with the use of timber, low-temperature and food-preservation stations, and the like. In such industries, the individual units find it difficult to keep abreast of research and development done elsewhere and to apply it in their particular circumstances. Hence for such industries networks of special research stations have arisen, associated with important information and field extension services. Some of these are associated also with professional training facilities for the sector. The land-grant colleges in the United States, for example, have played an exceedingly important role, not only in the improvement of agriculture, but also in the development of higher education.

Encouragement of industrial research

This topic will be dealt with below in the context of science and the economy (p. 69). It must be stressed here that nearly all governments have developed elaborate policies for the encouragement of research by and for industry, often particularly aimed at the small- and medium-sized firms, which suffer the same disadvantages with regard to research and its application as in the case of agriculture. The means adopted to encourage industrial research vary greatly from country to country and include the provision of fiscal incentives, direct subsidy, research and development contracts, government purchase in accordance with carefully devised specifications.

and the support of industrial research facilities. In Britain, the research association scheme has been the main mechanism employed. Within this, firms in a particular sector have been encouraged by exhortation and direct financial contribution to band together to create research institutions to undertake work of importance to the industry as a whole. This system has been much criticized for encouraging research and development work which, belonging to all, gives little competitive advantage to any individual firm. This is not a completely fair argument, since many of the associations have done much to raise the general technological level of their industry. In recent years there has been an attempt to meet the criticism by encouraging the associations to undertake contract research or development for individual firms in addition to their general programmes for the industry as a whole.

The research association system has been emulated in some of the British Commonwealth countries, and in the Netherlands, through TNO, a similar system has arisen. In countries with smaller numbers of firms in each sector, the system would hardly be viable since it could not be expected to provide a reasonable threshold of research effort. In Norway, for example, this problem is met through an industrial laboratory which provides general facilities of instrumentation, libraries, and workshops, where firms can separately or together have facilities for particular work or continuing programmes.

Apart from the general value to industry of the results of research undertaken in such associations, they have an important function in transmitting scientific and technological information in a highly selected and relevant form to the individual firms. This may in reality be their main influence, together with that of inducing individual firms to employ some technical staff, if not to undertake research, at least to create technical services and hence help to raise the technological level and awareness of the enterprise.

New major technologies

The development of nuclear power as a by-product of the atomic bomb became an important government commitment from the outset, not only because of security needs but also as a consequence of the large capital requirements for energy developments of an entirely novel type for which traditional industry was not yet ready.

This led to the creation of bodies such as the United Kingdom Atomic Energy Authority. Very soon, however, countries such as the United States and Britain started to off-load much of the development work to industry. In nearly all countries, however, national nuclear energy laboratories were created, even in many of the less industrialized countries, as a result of the American 'Atoms for Peace' programme. A somewhat similar path has been followed with regard to space research. In other fields such as computer development, the main task has been left to industry although at times government encouragement and subsidy has been given to the formation of consortia of industrial firms. As technology becomes more sophisticated and costly, government involvement in the development process—at least financially—seems inevitable. In Japan, for example, where the relationships between government and industry are particularly subtle and intimate, industry has indicated that government leadership and finance will be essential in the development stage of the next generation of equipment in a number of fields.

Medical research

Although a large proportion of medical research is undertaken in universities and their medical schools, many governments support the work of medical research councils, central research institutions, and specialized research centres. The National Institute of Health (NIH) in the United States is a comprehensive example of the national medical research organization, and for many years it also financed research projects, not only in America but in many other countries.

Social science research

The great upsurge of research activity since the end of the Second World War was supported mainly on the results to be expected from the physical sciences, and both economics and the behavioural sciences received much less support. Even economics, which has had such an important role in government during the last few decades, has not been able to mount research programmes commensurate with those of the natural sciences and engineering. As it becomes clearer that both economic and social elements of contemporary problems are inextricably intertwined with scientific and technological considerations, there has been a recent trend towards the creation of social science research councils and an increasing funding of individual projects. In many countries, however, the lack of research funds for such subjects makes it difficult to provide a continuity of career opportunity so that for the behavioural disciplines in particular, a scientific community such as that which operates internationally for the natural sciences as yet hardly exists.

Science and development

Recently, a new function has been added to the science responsibilities of governments, namely help to the less developed countries of the world through transfer of technology, and in solving their economic problems and those of life in the tropical environment. The great proportion of scientific research undertaken in the world takes place in the minority of industrialized countries, yet it is the others, struggling upwards from economic subsistence, that have a real need for technological help. Many of the countries which are donors of aid have research and development programmes in this field.

Hitherto much of this has consisted in the transmission of particular techniques, in relation to highly specific problems, but more recently a tendency can be discerned which regards science and technology as an agent of development. In most of the industrially advanced countries the organization for development aid, which may have a science component, has only a remote connection with national science programmes and policies.

International research co-operation

International research has become important in depth and extent since the end of the Second World War—both because of the importance of investigations in a number of fields where the environment cannot be constrained within national frontiers (for example, oceanography, meteorology, problems of arid territories, etc.) and also in a number of rapidly advancing fields where the equipment costs are beyond the resources of all but the largest nations (for example, high-energy physics, radio-astronomy, space research). The problems of international research co-operation are discussed below (see p. 80). National contributions to such research are normally a direct charge on governments, although in some international research schemes national participation is through learned societies in receipt of government subventions. For smaller, scientifically advanced countries, contribution to the work of intergovernmental scientific organizations can represent a significant proportion of their total research expenditure.

The wide range of research activities sketched above has in nearly all cases grown gradually in response to specific needs rather than within a framework of deliberate policy. Irrespective of economic level or structure, of political ideology or state of developments, governments have assumed, hardly realizing it, the major role in supporting scientific developments, maintaining their own laboratories, recruiting their own research staffs, and accepting responsibility, however ill-defined, for future development in a competitive world. Scientific education and research expenditure in many countries now amount to a sizeable proportion of the national income, yet it is only recently that such expenditures have come to be recognized as a necessary investment for the future and not merely as a cultural cost or as a problem-solving device. As the extent of national scientific effort grows, the more necessary does it become for governments to scrutinize expenditure and establish priorities. Consequently, both within the parliamentary apparatus and through research councils and foundations of the administrations, there is an increasing attempt to establish a balance of effort and a sense of priority. In most cases, this as yet hardly amounts to a science policy. Research policy it may be, but until research is conceived as an organic element in the totality of national policy, a motive force in the development of the economy and society, articulated with economic, social, cultural, and other aims, it is not science policy in any comprehensive sense. Such a policy implies not only the organization and support of research but stresses its application. It is inherently concerned with the linkage of the possibilities of new knowledge, whether domestic or imported, in the natural or the social sciences, with the achievement of national goals.

Steps towards policy

3

The allied governments' experience during the Second World War of the contributions both of research and of the operational analysis of practical problems had convinced them that science should have a constructive role in the rebuilding of Europe and in the affairs of societies at peace. It was obvious that many of the problems of research organization, programme co-ordination, relations between science and government, the difficulties of translating scientific discovery into technological hardware, and many others encountered during the war would persist within the civil economy. But it would be necessary to create new structures and new policies to meet the completely new objectives.

In the United States the debate began even before the end of hostilities, but many years were to elapse before a stable solution was adopted. Vannevar Bush, who had directed the Office of Scientific Research and Development (OSRD), submitted a report entitled *Science, the endless frontier* to President Roosevelt in July 1945. This is one of the classics of the literature of science policy. Bush had been greatly impressed by the fact that so many of the most successful technical developments of the war—the jet engine, new explosives, microwave radar, penicillin, DDT, and even the concept of the atomic bomb—had been developed on the basis of European fundamental research. The American genius for technological development, supported by an enormous industrialized capacity was able to exploit research discoveries made throughout the world extremely quickly, but there was a lack of fundamental research support and perhaps undue reliance on others for the basic ideas. This, he felt, should be rectified and a strong research network built up in America from which a new generation of technology would spring. The increase in the research population during the war and its excellent coupling with the process of development provided a very favourable resource; what was needed was policy and mechanism to exploit the potential. Bush therefore stressed the role of government in science and categorically stated that science was a proper and continuing concern of governments which had only just begun to take seriously the utilization of science for the national welfare. The main topics considered by the report were the importance of basic research, science within the government, industrial, medical and military research, the renewal of talent, and international relations in science. It recommended the creation of a National Research Foundation for the strategy and funding of American research and the Science Advisory Board to co-ordinate the Government's own research programmes.

At the end of the Second World War, OSRD was quickly liquidated and the universities reverted to their normal functioning but with greatly inflated student populations, thanks partly to the G.I. Bill of Rights. Wartime demands had multiplied the number of research workers and accustomed scientists to work on projects suggested by government agencies and to rely on public financial support which had now partially collapsed. In the absence of a research foundation the defence departments provided the only immediate source of money but there was some reluctance among the scientists after Hiroshima to continue to work on military proposals. The Office of Naval Research, however, took a very flexible approach and instituted a system of support for basic research linked only in the most indirect way to fields of knowledge and expansion of which would contribute to the long-term technical needs of the Navy Department. This greatly helped to fill the gap during the five years of legislative wrangling before the National Science Foundation was created.

A whole series of research Bills were submitted to Congress; there were interminable commission discussions. The National Science Foundation Bill, strongly supported by the scientific community, was indeed passed by both Houses of Congress in 1947, but was vetoed by President Truman on the grounds that the director, being elected by a board of independent persons, might be insufficiently responsive to the will of the people. An amended act was finally passed in May 1950. The National Science Foundation was duly created, essentially as a body concerned with the strategy and funding of fundamental research. Many feel that its preoccupations were over-academic and that too little attention was given to the over-all needs for research

in the attainment of national goals. Of late, it has turned more towards applied science and technological innovation, but over the
years it has been considerably overshadowed, particularly financially, by government science activities in the fields of nuclear energy
and space. Other elements of science policy soon evolved. A Federal
Council for Science and Technology was created to co-ordinate the
scientific work of the various government departments, as Bush had
suggested, and also the President's Science Advisory Council for
over-all problems of scientific policy and trends. The chairman of
these two bodies was the Scientific Advisor to the President, who
was the central figure in science policy determination. In Congress,
too, important progress has been made mainly through the House
Committee on science and astronautics which had gradually acquired competence and sophistication across the broad spectrum
of scientific development in relation to the public interest.

In Britain things went more smoothly at first. The Barlow Report,
immediately after the war, created the Scientific Civil Service. This
aimed to provide for scientists in government employ conditions and
propects conducive to creativity which the normal establishment
could hardly furnish. Furthermore it hoped to facilitate mobility between employment of scientists in government laboratories, universities, and the research associations through a transferable super-
annuation scheme, later rendered impotent as a result of inflation.
More important was the setting-up in 1947 of the Advisory Council
for Scientific Policy (ACSP) as a complement to the Defence Science
Committee, with Sir Henry Tizard as Chairman of both bodies and
with the two secretariats in adjacent accommodation in the Cabinet
offices. This arrangement enabled one man to see the totality of both
the British scientific and political scenes and, since his appointment
was on a ful-time basis, Tizard was in daily contact with the Ministers. The ACSP reported to the Lord President of the Council, at
that time Mr. Herbert Morrison, who took a lively interest in its
work, as did several other members of the Cabinet. The first annual
report of the Council outlined coherent institutional proposals for
the government's civil science activities. It recognized that research,
including fundamental research, although to be regarded as a national investment, is one which yields its dividends only after a number of years and that research directed at national needs must therefore be conceived on a long-term basis and take account of new
scientific knowledge wherever it might arise. Such research can

provide new products and processes only after the long stage of technological development is complete. There is always a danger that research undertaken directly by a government for its own needs will be forced to respond too frequently to immediate issues and degenerate into a somewhat pedestrian, trouble-shooting activity. This is especially a trap in a country such as Britain, where there exist many mission-oriented government laboratories.

The ACSP recommended that the main thrust of government research should be concentrated, not in laboratories within the various ministries, but under the three research councils—the Agricultural and Medical Research Councils and the Department of Scientific and Industrial Research—which by that time had developed into a kind of colony of research boards on applied topics, in addition to their functions of funding basic research and of stimulating and supervising the research associations. These three bodies, like the ACSP itself, reported directly to the Lord President and hence interaction between them was expected to be relatively easy to achieve. The main objective was thus to ensure that long-range investigations would be undertaken without undue interruption and diversion as a result of the short-term technical preoccupations of the departments and of their changing policies. In this scheme, for example, road research came under the Road Research Laboratory of DSIR and not within the Ministry of Transport; building research under the corresponding DSIR board and not the Ministry of Works; medical research under the Medical Research Council and not the Ministry of Health; agricultural research under the Agricultural Research Council rather than the Ministry of Agriculture. It was accepted, of course, that Ministries such as Agriculture or Works would need their own applied research laboratories to tackle the more immediate problems. To complement the system and establish close relations between the research bodies and the users, it was proposed that each Ministry should appoint a Chief Scientist of high level in the hierachy (normally Deputy Secretary) who would be responsible for identification and formulation of the main problems of his sector to the solution of which research might contribute. He would take part as an assessor on the appropriate research council or board, communicate his departments' research needs to his colleagues on this body, and be responsible for the application of the results.

This advice from the ACSP was accepted in principle. In practice many of the departments did appoint chief scientists: Agriculture, Works, Fuel and Power, the Home Office, and even for a time the Scottish Office. It is significant that the advice was ignored by the Board of Trade and the Foreign Office.

These general arrangements functioned for a number of years and represented perhaps the nearest the country has ever approached to a coherent science policy. The main criticism of the system, essentially one levelled by the Rothschild Report, was that in placing responsibility for research too far from the user of its results, programmes could develop which were too theoretical, too long-term in their significance, and not close enough to practical needs. This is indeed one of the central dilemmas of science policy. Both short- and long-term approaches are necessary, and means must be provided to develop both in close interaction. It should be remembered, however, that in all political affairs, electoral pressures force the administration in power to face immediate problems visible to the public, so that long-term and often more fundamental issues may be sacrificed. Given the inherent long-term nature of the research and the development process, this can easily lead to an ineffectual use of a country's scientific resources.

The early work of the ASCP was by no means restricted to these problems of over-all policy and structure. Ministers sought its advice on some specific policy issue, for example, on the effect of nutritional levels on the output of heavy industry, which had some influence on the post-war rationing systems at a time when a drastic reduction of food imports would have been welcome in order to save hard currency. The Lord President also asked the Council to advise on the potential influence on levels of productivity in industry. The work done did much to stimulate the creation of the productivity movement in Britain and also, as we shall see, in Europe.

When the post-war Labour Government fell and the Churchill administration took over. Lord Cherwell was given a ministerial post and Tizard resigned as chairman of the two central research councils. The wartime incompatibility between these two major science advisers, so well described by C. P. Snow in his Harvard lectures, thus cast a shadow on peacetime development of British science. It is ironical that Tizard, who was politically a Conservative, could serve only under a Labour Government. After his resignation, the influence of the ACSP began to decline, partly because his eminent successor, Sir Alexander (later Lord) Todd, was appointed on a part-time basis and thus had much less continuity of contacts with the ministers and with the problems that faced them. Furthermore, he had no responsibility for defence research. Finally, the Trend Report appeared and the DSIR, which had grown very large and become somewhat bureaucratic, was split up. But this later phase in British science policy will be dealt with in later volumes of this series.

In the other European countries where there was a complete discontinuity between the wartime conditions and the new situation of science for peacetime reconstruction, it was necessary to build up the research infrastructure; broad policy considerations were for the future. In France the National Council of Scientific Research (CNRS) was built up within the Ministry of Education. In the Netherlands two research councils, one for fundamental research (ZWO) and another for applied research (TNO) were created with a form which combined some of the features both of the DSIR and the research associations. The Germans created a National Research Council (Deutsche Forschungsgemeinschaft), publicly financed but independently constituted, as well as a whole series of research institutes under the Max Planck Society. In Belgium and Scandinavia corresponding institutions arose.

4

Science policy: the international concern

The decade which followed the ending of the Second World War was one marked by a mixture of hope, desperation and idealism. It saw the creation of the United Nations Organization, the gigantic accomplishment of rebuilding Europe from the ruins, greatly aided by the Marshall Plan and the first striving towards an integrated Europe. It is not surprising, therefore, that governments should have turned to science, which had been so determinative in winning the war, as a potentially valuable element in building a new world. From the beginning, the United Nations Organization discussed the need to build up scientific research for the material transformation of society. Its Economic and Social Council considered a somewhat grandiose scheme for the creation of world scientific laboratories on topics such as brain research, computation, and also for the attack on regional problems such as those of the Hylean Amazon. Alas, little came of this: the schemes were too vague, too far from the realities of day-to-day politics, and too costly at a time when physical reconstruction demanded all the available capital.

However, science, thanks largely to Joseph Needham and Julian Huxley, found an honoured place in UNESCO, one of the specialized agencies of the United Nations Organization, which had originally been conceived in purely educational and cultural terms without any specific mention of science. Over the years, UNESCO has contributed greatly to the internationalization of science. From the outset it decided to give financial support to the International Council of Scientific Unions, which strengthened the scientists' own international organization sufficiently to permit the individual unions to work more effectively and make possible a number of important international research projects. UNESCO also acted as midwife in the creation of the European Council for Nuclear Research (CERN)— probably the most effective of intergovernmental scientific enterprises which made it possible for the countries of Europe to remain in the forefront of high-energy physics, from which they would otherwise have been largely excluded by its high cost. UNESCO also, although somewhat haltingly, created the International Computation Centre in Rome, which has had a much less clearly defined task. Other important activities of UNESCO had an applied slant, such as its work on the problems of arid and of humid tropical zones. Through its regional scientific offices, it also helped much in extending scientific thinking and documentation in the less developed areas of the world.

It is not surprising therefore that UNESCO should, within its broad scientific programmes, have concerned itself with problems of science policy. In this, it has naturally been strongly influenced by the nature of its membership. The great majority of members are countries that are in the process of development. Much help has been given to such countries in developing policies for research and in building-up their scientific infrastructure. UNESCO's attitude is well summarized in the important volume written by Jacques Spaey (1969) (then in charge of the science policy of Belgium) and his colleagues, acting as UNESCO consultants, which regards science as an agent of development and not just a cultural or service concomitant.

From the point of view of the industrialized countries, science policy has been given great importance by the Organization for Economic Co-operation and Development (OECD) and its precursor, the Organization for European Economic Co-operation (OEEC), the Marshall Plan Organization. OECD is an association of twenty-three industrialized countries of the market economy world: those of Western Europe, the United States. Canada, Japan, Australia, and New Zealand, with Yugoslavia as an associate—nations which produce nearly three-quarters of the world's scientific research and technological development. It is inevitable that problems of the linkage of science to national objectives should arise initially in a sophisticated manner in such countries where the cost of research and hence its choice and management are important, and where the impact of technology on society is most clearly apparent.

Scientific topics first appear on the agendas of the OEEC Council as early as 1949, when a working party on scientific and technical information reported. Its conclusions were in practically the same terms as those of the British Committee on Science and Productivity a few months earlier: in the short term, that of European reconstruction and capital shortage; research and technological innovation had little to offer immediately, but a decade later it would become of major importance and experiments in international research co-operation should be initiated immediately. On the other hand, the working party felt that there could be immediate gains from the introduction of a more scientific attitude in industry, in the use of operational research, scientific management, and the cultivation of productivity, quantitatively measured. The group of scientists who made these recommendations launched in fact the European Productivity Movement, with active centres in all the Member countries, soon to be emulated throughout the world. OEEC set up its own European Productivity Agency, and later on the Office of Scientific and Technical Personnel from which the OECD programmes in science and education developed.

It is a characteristic of OECD work on both science and education that it is conceived in terms of policy and of influencing the thinking of the Member countries, rather than as projects which are ends in themselves. Within the economic growth and development objectives of the Organization such work is designed to provide new knowledge, experiment, or demonstration which seek, in a strictly practical sense, to provide to the Member countries elements of experience which can be incorporated in the evolution of their national policies. (For a fuller description of this approach, see p. 59.)

By 1959 discussions on science within OECD were raising doubts as to the effectiveness of research effort of its members in relation to over-all national, and especially economic, objectives. In that year, the Secretary-General of the Organization invited Mr. Dana Wilgress, formerly Canadian Ambassador to OEEC and NATO, to undertake a study of the scientific organizations of the Member countries and of their major problems. Specifically he was asked: (i) to discuss with governmental, scientific, and industrial leaders the measures taken or planned to increase the scientific and technological resources of each Member country; (ii) to make those in high authority aware of the importance that scientific research and technological development was likely to have on the future economy; and (iii) to propose measures at the national or international level that would increase technological resources and favour establishment of common action for their more rational use.

Mr. Wilgress visited most of the OECD countries for discussion with ministers, senior science administrators, and others. He came away with a strong feeling that in most countries research had grown in a haphazard manner in relation to specific needs and was seldom considered in terms of its real potentiality and in a policy sense. He concluded that 'the full implications of the scientific revolution has not yet sunk into the consciousness of large sections of the population of Western European countries—they are loth to scrap their traditions. In particular they are reluctant to adapt their educational systems to the needs of science and technology.'

Wilgress produced confidential reports on the situation in each country and a general report (1965), in which he stressed the economic significance of science and the need for coherent policies. 'The first thing should be for each country to draw up a national science policy'. By this he meant essentially a resource investment policy which took into account the need for a suitable balance between fundamental and applied research, concentrating on science as the basis for technological innovation and economic growth, and which included international co-operation. Within OECD, Wilgress recommended that consideration of scientific affairs should be consolidated and that a small high-level advisory group of scientists should be constituted as a science policy group.

The Wilgress Report was received favourably by the OEEC Council. A few months later, when the transformation of OEEC to OECD had taken place and the function of science in the new Organization was again under discussion, its Secretary-General, in the spirit of the Wilgress Report, appointed an *ad hoc* group of independent scientists and economists to '. . . advise me on the policy issues of science and technology that are increasingly demanding attention from government and the scientific community as well as the long-term objectives of OECD in this field'.

The *ad hoc* group on science policy, under the chairmanship of Monsieur Pierre Piganiol, at that time chief scientist of the French Government, worked for about a year and in turn produced its report *Science and the policy of governments* (1961), which provided a starting-point for consideration of science policy as we now know it.

The Wilgress Report, made to an economic organization, stressed the importance of considering research in terms of application, particularly to industry. The *ad hoc* group likewise began their deliberations by examining the problems and opportunities of harnessing science and technology to the broad economic objectives of OECD, but their analysis went much further.

First, it was quickly agreed that there was a need to develop policies for the management of national research resources. Clearly science and technology become of policy concern to governments when the opportunity offered by expanding knowledge greatly outstrip the resources in money and skills available to exploit them, and when governments and parliaments have become the major supporters of research to an extent that the necessary resources represent a substantial fraction of the national budget. If there is more good science about than money to sustain it, priorities must be established and policy formulated. Furthermore, if substantial sums of public money are being spent on research and development and in the training of the requisite skills, governments have the duty to try to ensure that this is being used effectively and in the public interest. Allocation of resources both between different scientific specializations and between pure science aiming only at the extension of knowledge and oriented or applied research required for the development of new technology is extremely difficult. In the early 1960s, when talk of priorities in research began to be heard, the idea was utterly abhorrent to most scientists, who saw in it government control, bureaucratic constrains, and a dwindling of inspiration and creativity. It soon became apparent, however, even to the most enthusiastic specialists and in a situation of expanding research budgets, that the rapid extension of research activity and mounting costs of sophisticated equipment did necessitate a degree of choice. In practice, governments have responded wisely to this problem and have not attempted to become arbiters of what is good science. A sound governmental science policy will respect the values of scientific freedom and recognize the necessity of allowing, expecially in fundamental research, the established research worker to follow the lines of his own genius. Most governments have devoted a generous proportion of the national research budget to the support of free-choice fundamental research—some would say too much so. Similarly, in distributing grants and fellowships they have developed mechanisms whereby selection is made on the advice of panels of scientists—the so-called principle of judgement by peers.

Allocation of resources for research is, however, only one aspect of policy to ensure a strong scientific effort. Governments have had to take advice from the scientific community concerning organizational questions and on the type of environment conducive to a high sustained research creativity. The *ad hoc* group, bearing in mind these and other considerations, stressed the need for each country to develop both policies and mechanisms for the management and effectiveness of the science system as such, which they called 'policies for science'.

However, still broader issues emerge with regard to the application of research and the contributions which a scientific approach can make to the attainment of national objectives. After all, the provision of substantial public funds for research is justified to the taxpayer on the expectations of equally substantial contributions to the welfare of a nation in general and not only through the cultural and conceptual advances which arise from fundamental research. As the group expressed it:

The term 'science policy' is ambiguous. It too often connotes only a policy limited to the needs of science *per se* and excludes the effects of science and technology on the full spectrum of national policies in such disparate fields as agriculture and industry, defence, education and domestic and foreign political affairs.

This argues that government policies in every field are, at least in principle, capable of improvement and refinement through the application of new knowledge derived from scientific research. This was, of course, completely accepted with regard to defence, where the successful application of research generated much of the support for increased science budgets, but was much less clear in other fields, including the economy. One of the main points of the report was to enlarge the spectrum to include the potential of science to assist in the formulation of social, education, and manpower policies of foreign aid, health, transportation, and the like. This aspect of science policy was termed by the group 'science for policy'.

The essential contribution of *Science and the policy of governments* was to review the total concern of governments with science and to make for the first time a clear distinction between the two faces of science policy—policy for science and science for policy— which, although closely interactive, require separate consideration.

The recommendations of the report were first that each government should consider setting up some central mechanism to discuss science policy in this broad sense and to advise ministers accordingly, and secondly a call to OECD to convene a meeting of ministers responsible for science policy or organization in the Member countries to continue and deepen the debate.

5

Ministers discuss science

The Piganiol Report was duly accepted by the OECD Council and preparations started for the first conference of science ministers which met in October 1963. (For a full account of this meeting, see *Ministers talk about Science*, OECD, Paris, 1965). There was some opposition to the idea of holding such a meeting in OECD because of the essentially economic nature of the Organization. Despite the building-up of national scientific institutions, only a small minority possessed, as yet, central mechanisms for science policy—a topic which, if discussed at all, was generally a matter for ministers of education and hence considered in terms of cultural policy. In such circumstances there was a fear that consideration of science in an economic body might subordinate it to industrial needs.

While *Science and the policy of governments* was regarded as the background paper for the meeting as a whole, three reports were prepared to introduce specific broad issues, namely national science policies, international research co-operation and science, economic growth and government policy. The meeting was thus conceived as providing a *tour d'horizon* and exchange of national experience to enable ministers to deepen their understanding of the issues and formulate more clearly the main problems of science policy which they would have to face. As such, it led to no dramatic recommendations; its communiqué was anodyne, but it had a deep influence on many countries in their understanding of the problems and greatly assisted in securing the implementation of the second recommendation of the Piganiol Report, the creation of central science policy mechanisms and, in a number of cases, the appointment of science ministers to head them.

With regard to national science policies, the background paper, the descriptions of existing national situations, and the debate itself illustrated the disparity of approach of the moment. Only a few countries—Belgium, France, the United Kingdom, and the United States—had studied the problem at all comprehensively and made arrangements accordingly. Germany and Sweden were at an earlier stage of development but had some beginnings of a science policy mechanism. Most of the others showed a recognition of the need for some sort of concerted action in the area but had taken few steps to create a mechanism. The most direct and systematic approach to national science policy was that of Belgium, whose Prime Minister (and Minister of Science) was Monsieur Théo Lefèvre, who was elected Chairman of the meeting. Under his authority, the National Science Policy Council of Belgium had cognizance over all aspects of the problem and was empowered to propose the reorientation or reorganization of relevant activities throughout the government structure. A detailed and continuing inventory of scientists and of research projects throughout the country had been compiled as well as the creation of a central and comprehensive science budget. An attempt was also being made to determine priorities for applied research explicitly in conformity with economic criteria.

This question of the merits and weaknesses of establishing central national research budgets was hotly debated at the meeting and for several years thereafter. Belgium developed a functional science budget, distinct from traditional sectoral categories, in order to make better use of it as a management tool. The French science budget similarly was a collection of those parts of the budgets of the various departments relating to research and development functions. Other countries, such as Britain and the United States, have rejected the concept of a central science budget, arguing that in each sectoral budget—for example, for health care—the research element is essentially a matter of opportunities opening at the particular time and has to be balanced with capital, operational, administration, service, and other aspects of the sectoral activity. From this point of view, a central research budget, conceived as a sort of cake of human and financial resources, which is cut into slices of different sizes by a bargaining process between the departmental claimants, seems quite artificial. These and many other issues were discussed in detail. There was strong advocacy of fundamental research and its need for academic freedom, a particularly sensitive matter at this time when the encroachment of governmental intervention and priority determination was greatly feared. At the same time the need for industrial research was stressed and the need for consistent criteria for its support and encouragement. The need for better statistics for research and development was underlined, as was that to improve systems of scientific and technical information. The scope of the term 'science' was discussed and it was agreed that the first meeting of ministers should concentrate on the natural sciences and technology but later discussions should include the social sciences and the humanities, and in particular there should be consideration of the role of the social sciences in the policy-making process. Finally, there was a minor terminological squabble as to whether the term should be 'science policy' or 'scientific policy'. Lord Hailsham, the British minister, pleaded strongly for the latter on grammatical grounds but science policy received the consensus. This decision was probably wise: little policy is as yet scientific, but we shall return to this topic later.

The other two topics have been the subject of debate throughout the whole series of ministerial meetings and will be discussed in more detail in later chapters. With regard to international research co-operation, there was at the time, and indeed still is, a good deal of disquiet concerning the rapid and apparently random proliferation of international organizations dealing with science—both intergovernmental and independent, general and highly specialized. In preparation for the meeting OECD had compiled a repertoire (*International scientific organizations*, 1963) of the main organizations in the field, with a short history of the development of such activities and as analysis of the main problems which is, alas, still valid. The ministers noted that international scientific co-operation has become an increasingly important element in scientific effort, partly because so many subjects are inherently appropriate for co-operation, being concerned with such topics as astronomy, the weather, the oceans, or diseases, which recognize no national frontiers, and also because of the arising of 'big sciences' which demand installations and instruments which are beyond the means of most countries. However, this development, particularly vigorous during the past few decades, had not evolved within any policy framework and in many—if not most—instances was linked only vaguely to national science policies and, indeed, over-all national needs. The ministers stressed the desirability of linking their national and international research policies, recognizing the need for analysis and evaluation of experience of international research schemes, including the provision of comparable data to allow assessment of the costs and benefits to the participating countries.

Discussion of the importance of science and technology in economic and social development marked the beginning of a long debate which still continues. Looking back to 1963, the approach to science as a national investment and as an element of growth seems somewhat naïve, but it did recognize the operation of a number of basic factors and enabled the issues to be formulated at least tentatively. Among other conclusions was an invitation to OECD to start work on the establishment of comparable statistics of national expenditure and manpower concerning research and development.

Before they dispersed, the ministers agreed to meet again in two years' time. Their second meeting took place in January 1966 under the chairmanship of Monsieur Peyrefitte, then Minister of Science for France. This meeting was in many ways a continuation of the first in that many of the same themes were taken up and discussed in greater depth. An important difference was the attendance of a number of new science ministers whose posts had been created in the meantime.

In preparation for the meeting, special studies had been made of the role of fundamental research and of the social sciences with regard to the policies of governments. In both cases these were prepared by groups of eminent scientists acting as individuals and not as representatives of governments. Fundamental research was regarded as a long-term national investment, intimately linked to the educational system and regarded as important for maintaining the vitality of teaching at advanced levels. Equally, however, it gives rise to, and is to some extent stimulated by, the process of technological innovation. Ministers recognized the need for each country to sustain sufficient research activity to provide a threshold of awareness of world scientific progress as well as of advanced skills, without which the transfer of technology is unlikely to be effective. A number of particular schemes were advocated, particularly the concentration of effort around outstanding research leaders within specific countries in order to generate centres of excellence of critical magnitude. Equally the linking of such centres within a European network was advocated but very little practical action resulted.

The discussion of the role of the social sciences was even less constructive. The report had analysed the situation well, particularly of the behavioural sciences, and had stressed the need for policies to make possible sustained research and career structures, the need for increased resources from governments, and for inclusion of the social scientist in the natural science policy-making bodies. The ministers gave some rather general support to the proposals, but it was clear that these were premature.

During the second ministerial meeting, understanding of the nature of the relationship between science and the economy became much clearer as well as of the need for governments to establish policies for stimulating technological innovation, including fiscal measures, the support of industrial research, and the operation of information and advisory services, development contracts, and government procurement.

The most important debate of this meeting centred upon the topic of resources for research and development. The problem of allocating limited resources between competing claims was regarded as one of the most difficult problems of science policy. The greatest interest was aroused, however, by the recognition of disparities in levels of research and development activity between the various Member countries of OECD and particularly between the United States and the most highly industrialized countries of Europe. OECD had commissioned Professor Christopher Freeman (now at the University of Sussex) and his colleague Miss A. Young to make a comparative study of national efforts on research and development in terms of both finance and manpower as far as the existing meagre statistical data would allow. Their report (Freeman and Young 1965) provided the basis for a highly controversial debate, particularly between representatives from Europe and the U.S.A. It was quickly realized that the available data were quite insufficient to provide a firm basis of comparison of national efforts and that, more importantly, too little was known of the influence of research and development or of governmental policies for such activity on the competitiveness of different industrial sectors. The ministers therefore recommended that OECD should intensify its work on establishing comparability in the gathering of statistics on research and development and of its analysis of the results of the first international statistical year for the topics. Furthermore, they decided that, subject to the completion of studies which OECD would undertake, they would devote their next meeting, or a large part of it, to the problems of disparity of research and development effort betwen countries, its influence on industry and trade, and related problems. This launched the series of studies which soon became well-known under the title *The technological gap*. The culmination of this work will be described in Chapter 8.

6
National science policies: some issues and options

The term 'policy' connotes both deliberate intention and coherence. As we have seen, the great expansion of scientific activity during the last two decades has been sporadic and uneven, growing in response to the general recognition of the value of research, its importance as a means of solving specific problems, and also as a result of the successful pressure of scientists concerned with a number of fashionable fields of investigation. Science policy, therefore, is only now striving towards coherence and consists of a somewhat disparate set of problems and issues. During this period, research resources have mainly been justified by their potential contributions to three major objectives—defence, national prestige, and economic growth—although, of course, relatively much smaller programmes have been in operation for health, public works, education, and so on. It is not surprising that in countries with large military commitments the correspondingly large research and development effort has been created and managed somewhat apart from civil research, not only for security reasons but because of an essential need for close working between the scientist and the user of his products. The situation has in most places been much the same for space research and nuclear energy.

As far as the economic objectives of research are concerned, science policy is essentially policy for the development of technology. It goes far beyond the simple policy for science aspect, i.e. the creation of an environment in which science can flourish, the necessary manpower provided, and choices made among a wide variety of scientific and technological projects. It extends from resource allocation to the encouragement by governments of technological development and strategy to secure high levels of industrial growth.

Until recently, science has been to some extent a *chasse gardée* to which parliaments voted resources with relatively little questioning on the simple assumption that research is a good thing and more research would solve more problems. Decisions were taken without much serious conflict in the easy circumstances of continuous expansion, which was so rapid and sustained that it came to be regarded almost as an inevitable phenomenon, virtually free from the problems of political choice. For the OECD countries during this period of euphoria, the initial thrust of science policy was essentially that of raising the level of R and D expenditure, as a fraction of the gross national product (GNP) of the individual countries, towards the level of that of the United States. In this process both governments and scientists regarded R and D as a valuable national investment in its own right, virtually without consideration of the content, provided it was sufficiently creative and sophisticated, and with only superficial consideration of the coupling of the research process to the operational problems faced by the member governments.

In the last few years, however, national objectives have been changing. Military, space, nuclear, and other large public research programmes have been tailing off, much more searching questions have been asked concerning the objectives of new research projects, problems of accountability have been raised and, in general, science has entered a period of disenchantment. Of course, other goals susceptible to research attack are appearing, such as the prevention of environmental deterioration, better health care, and education, but in most cases the social aims are far from being clearly formulated and politically agreed to the extent that the demands they will make on research can be seen. Furthermore, most of the new socially oriented programmes of research are of an order of magnitude less than the large technology programmes of recent years and are of a nature so different that they cannot be undertaken by a mere switch of research workers from one field to another. This may well lead to a hiatus between the running-down of certain large-scale R and D projects of a 'hardware' type in some fields, with a consequent unemployment of engineers, before new programmes calling for a quite different mix of disciplines, including the social sciences, are established to meet new objectives.

Such changes in the goals, to the attainment of which research may have much to contribute, will inevitably modify our understanding of what science policy means. The nature of these goals and changes will be discussed in some detail later, but their shadow is already cast on many of the issues of science policy now to be considered.

The agencies responsible for science policy vary greatly. Many of them have in fact no responsibility for research related to defence, and hence this important use of R and D resources has little direct influence on their general consideration of policy, although indirectly it may greatly influence their budgets and the availability of scientific manpower. In some countries again, science policy is quite unrelated to national efforts to encourage industrial innovation and improvement, and concentrates on the allocation of resources to fundamental research. While it is useful to distinguish between science for the production of new knowledge as distinct from technology (which is the application of knowledge to produce new products useful to man, or new methods of production), it is increasingly accepted that science and technology, despite their different methods and constraints, form part of a single system both within national frameworks and on a universal scale. Again, in some countries the training of scientists, which at a high level of skill still relies on apprenticeship by doing research under the supervision of an experienced research leader, is the responsibility of the educational system with its guidelines formulated quite independently of central science policy considerations. It should be noted also that in many agencies, even within research oriented policies, coverage is only partial. Some of these may concentrate, for example, on the 'big sciences', which necessitate substantial investment in equipment; many ignore the social sciences; in others whole sectors of civil research such as health or urban problems are neglected in favour of areas which feed large technological or prestige ventures. To sum up: in the past, different areas of science policy have often, if naturally, been treated independently of one another with only superficial attempts at co-ordination. This has often resulted in insufficient resources being given to interface subjects which are often points of important scientific growth. For example, many biological and biochemical topics too easily fall between funding institutions concerned with medical and natural science research respectively.

The problems of structure

Only a few of the central issues of science policy can be discussed here. Among these, the structural problems stand out, and indeed few countries are satisfied with the institutional arrangements they have made for dealing with the policies, strategies, and management of the national scientific effort. This is demonstrated by the fact that the average OECD country has made several fundamental changes in the science structure during the past decade, while the debate about their efficiency still continues. Not only is the topic 'science' ill-defined, but it ranges over a broad continuum from education at one end to agricultural, industrial, and defence production as well as social change at the other. This continuum of activity is too vast to fall under the authority of a single minister or a single department. The problem, therefore, is how to cut it up into manageable segments. In some countries, as at present in Britain, the cut has been made in the middle, with education and fundamental research under one department and applied research and technology associated with industry and trade in another. No matter how good the co-ordinating mechanism may be, this has the disadvantage of separating science from technology, two subjects which must develop in symbiosis if each is to be finally successful in contributing to the national wellbeing. The result of such division can well be a technology too narrowly related to the immediate preoccupations of government departments and a basic research effort insufficiently concerned with the long-term needs of society. In other countries, such as Austria and Germany, an area of separate ministerial responsibility has been carved out in the middle, with higher education and most categories of research, fundamental as well as applied, leaving general and technical education on one side and technological development and industry on the other. Problems of articulation still remain. Still other countries, such as Norway and Sweden, while operating central boards or councils to survey science policy and resource needs as a whole, leave the detailed programming to a series of research councils for specific sectors. This is not too unlike the British system, in which most government scientific activity is in the hands of research councils or of government laboratories whose programmes are developed on the advice of boards of individual scientists and users, whatever the departmental application of the laboratory or research council may be. The existence of such councils can go far to ensure that long-term possibilities are not ignored and that more radical scientific solutions to problems are considered. Many, on the other hand, feel that unless the work of such councils is in intimate and continuous contact with the potential users of their research product, their work will tend to be too unrealistic and function merely as an extension of the 'pure' research activities of the university.

Centralization versus pluralism

This is, however, but one dimension of the problem. A related topic is the difficult issue of the proper balance between centralized policies for science and technology considered as a single aggregate, and sectoral policies of economic or social objective served by science and technology. There is no single or final solution to the problem, but any system of science policy must always strive towards a viable equilibrium which involves a blend of both the centralized and sectoral approaches.

A dominantly centralized model has been adopted by a number of European countries such as Belgium and France, not merely in terms of budgetary practice as described on p. 39, but with regard to the planning or organization of research and development. None of them follows it completely in practice. In this system all the resources of government research are provided through a central authority, generally a ministerial committee presided over by the Prime Minister or his representative and advised by an advisory council of scientists. This mechanism attempts to cut the scientific cake into slices of different size for each of the claimant ministries or agencies according to their needs or possibly their political influence. The approach attempts to centralize not only resource allocation but also decision-making in a broad sense, while leaving the detailed planning and conduct of research decentralized. It has the advantage of facilitating a total over-all policy for technical activity, which minimizes abrupt shifts disrupting research continuity. It also relates research more directly to over-all national objectives, at least in theory, and makes evident the relative weights of national priorities and changes between them. It has the weakness that the resource-availability in a particular field is decided by bargaining and compromise between claimants at a high level, somewhat remote from the realities of scientific work and its exploitation, rather than justified by scientific promise in competition with all the other potential claimants for investment resources of the sector. This can also lead to over-rigid bureaucratic decision and control, to ignoring the possibilities of new lines of research, and, in general, to conservatism.

The United States system has emphasized the pluralistic approach, with total (not merely research) resources being made available directly to the various sectors such as defence, space, agriculture, or health, and the appropriate R and D levels profitable for the particular sector determined in competition with capital and service expenditures in the same field. The over-all national science policy (and budget) therefore becomes the sum of the sectoral policies (and budgets) determined independently. In the United States the individual sectoral agencies present their proposals after discussion with the Bureau of the Budget, and these are argued separately and severally with the Congressional Appropriation Committees. A central function of scanning the national scientific effort, looking at new problems and possibilities, was for many years, undertaken by the President's Scientific Advisory Committee, whose chairman (the President's Science Adviser) also chaired a Federal Council for Science and Technology which loosely co-ordinates the research activities of the various departments and agencies while attempting no real resource allocation between them. A great advantage of this approach was that research and development activity was more easily coupled with the real problems of the various sectors and with individual national goals. The results of relevant scientific research which is undertaken close to sectoral needs appear to be more quickly understood and accepted. The disadvantage of a strictly sectoral approach is, as we have seen, a tendency to ignore the longer-term problems which may not be immediate departmental preoccupations; also, in times of budgetary stringency, research is too easily sacrificed in favour of maintaining service and operational activities, the reduction of which would be politically damaging.

In the United States, with the levelling-off of the R and D budget in recent years and the general reassessment of national objectives for the research effort, the scientific community is looking with more favour at centralized models, even to the extent of proposing schemes for a central agency or department. At the same time, in some of the European countries until recently devoted to the centralized model, the trend is towards pluralism as the level of research resource rises.

Undoubtedly new concern with the broader problems of society will encourage the evolution of sectoral research policies for fields such as the environment, transportation, health care, urban affairs, education, etc. The problem of finding a blend between the two approaches to science policy will become more acute, but meanwhile most countries oscillate uncertainly between them. A recent OECD report, *Science, growth and society* (the Brooks Report, 1971), suggests that governments might have something to learn on this topic from the experience of some of the large science-based industrial firms which successfully operate their R and D activities by a mixture of centralization and decentralization. Such firms frequently have research units attached to their operational or product divisions to assist with the immediate problems of established production and agreed innovations; they often possess, in addition, a corporate laboratory responsible for scanning the new scientific possibilities of the world, responsible for longer-term research aimed at developing quick new products and processes in the future, and in general providing a general background of scientific and technological knowledge and stimulus for all the firm's activities and decisions. Some firms, such as Hitachi in Japan, go a step further: their central laboratory with its own budget for the more distant research possibilities also accepts contracts for R and D from the operating divisions, which enables particular research activities of these units to be undertaken with a continuity undisturbed by the trouble-shooting disruption so common in industrial laboratories. The Brooks Report suggested that such a model should be considered for R and D on the national level and, more specifically, that a proportion of the total funds should be allocated centrally to a scientific agency capable of rapid response to changing national goals and priorities, long-term horizons, and the development of an adequate knowledge base for the formulation of new objectives. Most of the funds for R and D, in this system, which would complement this central allocation would be derived, sector by sector, from the total operating funds of each. This would enable research to be done on short-term operating problems and effective coupling to be made between research and new needs.

Research policy or science policy

During the 1960s science was considered by the OECD countries as an independent variable of policy only loosely related to the total political and social context, in contrast to the view of the Marxist nations. This was the period in which the public attitude to science was optimistic, uncritical, and uncomplicated. If problems remained unsolved it was because there was too little research or because we did not know how to use it effectively. Technology policy was often viewed in much the same way as policies for fundamental research, and its investments were too readily regarded as good in themselves. It was not until more was known about the nature of technological innovation, with its complex of functions within which the research input is only one, that the autonomous approach to science and technology was seriously challenged. This will increasingly be the case as science and technology are directed more to the solutions of problems with large social and political components.

In effect, the science policy of most countries is as yet research policy and is confined to the financing of research considered as generally useful, but with little sense of the need for articulation with other elements of policy and hence with little direct impact on them. It is only in military, space, and nuclear research—fields which are in any case excluded from central science policy consideration in many countries—that real efforts have been made to link scientific and technical activities within a coherent perspective of policy, and hence where policy itself can be influenced through appreciation of hitherto ignored possibilities offered by new discovery. The generalization of such an approach will be the beginning of a true science policy.

Priorities and goals

Since the end of the Second World War, research priorities have been largely determined by objectives of defence, national prestige, or economic development rather than the needs of social change, abolition of poverty, better health services, and so on. On the whole, science and technology have been successful in meeting many of the specific goals, despite the unwanted side-effects which have accumulated in the process. This success was due to the fact that the targets were clear and a corpus of fundamental knowledge was already in existence and ripe for exploitation, or at least there was sufficient understanding of basic principles on which such knowledge could be developed. These same objectives are likely to remain valid during the next phase (military imperatives, alas, are always with us; our countries are committed to policies of continuing growth and prestige is a useful adjunct to foreign policy) although they are likely to decline in relative importance in the public and political view, unless the menace of major war appears. Science and technology for national security are therefore likely to continue to play a major role in science policy in the larger countries and to influence innovation even in the civilian sectors, while further development of 'hardware' technology and the fundamental research on which it is ultimately based will be sought for economic ends. However, many aspects of industrialized societies are approaching what the Brooks Report describes as the precursor of saturation. For example, with regard to certain categories of consumer goods, acceptable levels of pollution, total population and the size of urban conglomerations, traffic, absorption of information, even higher education, and perhaps the total number of people devoted to the uncovering of new knowledge through research. Likewise the move of employment from the primary and secondary to the tertiary sector is likely to quicken, and with it will come a shift from the production of privately marketable goods to the production of public goods in the form of services collectively supplied by the public sector.

This change in the goals of society is already beginning to produce an imperative need to reassess the place of science—both in general cultural terms and in the manifestation of new technology of the 'hardware' and 'software' types. But this will not be easy. The social goals are not simple to formulate precisely because they rest on systems of values which are shifting rapidly, are highly political in their significance, and on which it will be difficult to obtain consensus. Unless the goals are clear, research to meet them will be difficult to select and to apply, as compared with the simple objectives of the past. Furthermore, the setting of merely tactical priorities on the basis of social goals is likely to be wasteful and self-defeating unless science and its policies are involved both in the goal-setting process and in strategic choice of broad fields for selective emphasis.

It will have to be recognized, too, that national objectives will seldom be completely compatible with each other. Even with the limited situation today, we notice both positive and negative influences from research towards one group of objectives on other policy areas. Thus we talk of the 'spin-off' from military research to the civilian economy (a desirable phenomenon which should be optimized) and the unwanted side-effects of technology on the environment (a negative and even limiting factor). As the range of national goals expands—to the attainment of which science and technology will contribute—these problems of inter-goal conflict and reinforcement will increase both in magnitude and complexity. One of the most important tasks for research may well be to understand the workings of these interactions more clearly and to elaborate the conceptual basis.

We are still only at the beginning of the reassessment of the role of science in the next phase of social development, but it is already certain that many new and difficult issues will be presented to science policy-makers. They will have to be much more deeply involved in the setting of national goals, the priorities between them, and the strategies necessary, if the goals themselves are to be realistic in the sense that they take account of the potentialities and limitations of new research, and if the system of science and technology is to respond effectively.

Ministerial responsibility for science

In the early 1960s recognition by governments of the importance of science and technology led, as we have seen, to the appointment, of a number of ministers responsible for science policy. Their functions vary from country to country, as do the organizations of which they are in charge, and change just as frequently. There are, in fact, science ministers of two kinds, which in British parlance were formerly categorized as ministers *of* science and ministers *for* science. *Ministers of science* are those in charge of executive departments with detailed responsibilities for allocation of resources and for operations. Thus, in Austria or Germany there are ministers of science and higher education with functional responsibility for universities as well as research. *Ministers for science,* on the other hand, are staff ministers, supported by a small secretariat to provide the basic statistical and other data and analyses of the problems. This was the British style for a number of years, initially with the Lord President of the Council as Minister for Science, until the function was given independent ministerial status under Lord Hailsham. The succeeding administrations abolished the post and created an executive Minister for Education and Science as well as the parallel ministerial post for technology. In France too, for nearly a decade, a staff minister representing the Prime Minister was responsible for science, but in that country also the function was later fused with those of the Minister of Industry who became Minister for Industry and Science. He and his chief scientists, however, retained an interdepartmental staff responsibility for French science and technology as a whole. In the United States there is no separately designated secreary for science with departmental responsibilities, but until recently the President's science advisor had a central role. The present situation in Canada is interesting in that the Trudeau administration has shown concern with the existence of a growing number of important national activities which fall fractionally across a wide range of departmental responsibilities without any actual point of policy integration. A Bill was passed by the Canadian Parliament in 1971 to rectify this my making possible the creation of a limited number of posts for 'horizontal' staff Ministers of State with the right to sit in the Cabinet. The first of these to be appointed was a Minister for Urban Affairs, and the second a Minister for Science. This post differs from earlier appointments in that the coordination and integration function is heavily stressed and the possibility given for substantial staff support to make this a reality.

With the new concepts of science policy now being developed, recognition of the need to evolve policies in intimate relationship with economic, social, and other policies throws the whole question of the status, need for, range of responsibilities, and political importance of science ministers wide open for discussion.

Decision-making and participation

The development of a realistic research, if not a science, policy, made it necessary for governments initially to seek participation of the scientific community in the detailed operation of their scientific programmes. In some countries long tradition had given a substantial advisory role to the academies and learned societies. This was particularly the case with the Royal Society in Britain, which had a long tradition of advising the government on scientific matters and even, as in the case of the National Physical Laboratory, a place in the determination of programmes. As government scientific activities expanded, it became increasingly difficult for the academies with their strictly limited resources to fill this role effectively. In most cases they have relinquished the function, reluctantly, but almost completely, reverting to the normal learned society activities as their main function.† Governments, on the other hand, usually included independent scientists as individuals on their science policy and research councils and depended greatly on the advice of scientific specialists in the detailed assessment of research proposals through the previously-mentioned system of judgement by peers. In two cases, that of the Royal Academy of Engineering Sciences of Sweden and the National Academy of Sciences of Washington, a real attempt has been made to develop a collective statesmanship in science above the vested-interest pressures of groups of specialists enthusiastic to secure greater resources for their own fields. The Swedish Academy has had a significant role in making the Swedish Government aware of new possibilities offered by research, of gaps in the existing research structure, and of the need for effective coupling of research with application, and has in a number of cases given rise to new research institutions. The National Academy of Science in the United States has been successful in providing Congress with a second opinion on many scientific issues to be compared with that of the administration's own scientific advisers, but since the individuals concerned are themselves frequently members of the President's Science Advisory Council or the National Science Foundation Board, the advice is seldom very divergent. It is interesting to note, however, that on a number of occasions the Academy has been invited to undertake, under contract, special studies on behalf of Congress.

In two countries of the OECD group, more institutional approaches have been made to the problem of participation of individual scientists in science policy determination. In Japan, the Science Council is a democratically constituted body with a secretariat in the Prime Minister's Office. Each practising scientist in the country has a vote for the membership of the Council and its sectoral committees. In practice this has not worked out well. The scientists on the whole have political opinions considerably to the left of the Japanese Government in power since the American occupation, and the Council's advice is by no means always acceptable. This is somewhat embarrassing to the Government, and as a consequence advice is frequently obtained by assimilating acceptable

†In the Soviet Union and other socialist countries, the acadamies of science have become strong official bodies with a major role in national science, as distinct from technological activity.

members of the Science Council on to the various government scientific committees as individuals. The Yugoslav experiment is much too recent to evaluate: it consists first of all in a delegation of responsibility for science policy, as of the other functions, from the Federal Government to the Republics and, at the regional level, of universal participation of the scientists in the policy-making process. This has, initially at least, given rise to a degree of enthusiasm on the part of individuals, who feel identified with the policies to which they have subscribed. In the political homogeneity of the country this may prove to be more effective than in Japan in providing through broad and active participation a counter to the inefficiencies of what appears from outside to be an excessive decentralization.

The place of a parliament in relation to the national support for science raises many issues, not merely concerning accountability for expenditure of taxpayers' money, but also because of the difficulty individual members have in understanding the varied, complex, and highly specialized issues related to science and technology which they are frequently called on to judge. Until recently, many of these decisions have been taken on faith, but with the contemporary questioning of science and perception of its negative as well as positive aspects, the task of the parliamentarian becomes ever more difficult. One of the problems is how to assess the value of research where practical application may appear many years later. Inputs are easily measured in terms of R and D expenditure or manpower data; outputs are often indirect, long delayed, and impossible to measure quantitatively. In several countries attempts have been made to bring together scientists and parliamentarians for discussion aimed at mutual appreciation of each other's problems. The Parliamentary and Scientific Committee in Great Britain is the prototype of this approach, emulated in several other countries. In other cases, the various political parties have their own science groups. In general, however, success in tackling these problems has depended on the emergence of one or two individuals in the elected assembly who, either by background or inclination, have taken a real and intelligent interest in scientific problems. The best example is perhaps once again that of the United States, where former Congressman Daddario succeeded in guiding a congressional subcommittee which accumulated a great deal of knowledge and wisdom on science policy matters and sought expert advice as required. In that country an excellent information service has been supplied through the Library of Congress to provide its members with factual material concerning scientific matters of legislative interest, and it is now proposed to create directly under Congress a centre for the assessment of the social as well as economic consequences of various technological alternatives. By such means, debates on, for example, space, defence, or supersonic civilian aircraft have reached a high degree of sophistication. At a recent conference of scientists and parliamentarians convened by the Council of Europe (1972), it was evident that parliamentarians are increasingly aware of, and interested in, the newer and especially the social problems of science policy, and there was a demand for science information facilities, possibly organized collectively, for the use of the European parliaments.

With regard to science and parliament, Yugoslavia has once again taken an original direction. Both at Federal level and in the constituent Republics, in addition to the political chamber of the Assembly, chambers have been constituted for economic activities, health and welfare, social questions, and science and education. The science chambers are not, as it were, sub-groups of representatives of the political house, but consist of representatives of science and education directly elected by those professionally active in science and education. The science chamber has the right to propose pertinent legislation, agree it on substantive grounds, and introduce it in the political chamber. The chambers also have certain rights of veto concerning legislation originating in other chambers which has important elements relative to their interests.

Organization and creativity

The success of a national science effort depends not only on its over-all structures and political coupling, but still more on the quality of the research accomplished. The creativity of research is therefore a basic requisite for which the national science policy must find propitious conditions. In the universities, where the freedom of the research scientist to choose his own themes and methods is habitual, individuals can emerge, and their creativity is maintained by exposure of successive waves of research students, thus ensuring permanent cross-fertilization between experienced minds and those of younger people, which are open and penetrating even though they have not yet had the opportunity to mature. In other forms of institution, including government laboratories with a much more static research population, there is a greater tendency for even the first-class researcher to become stale as the years pass. In general therefore the university environment is considered best for fundamental research.

A large proportion of the fundamental research undertaken today is essentially oriented research, aimed at opening up new fields of knowledge required for application. Even here there is considerable advantage in bringing the themes to university research schools with reputations in the field in question and relying on the free-choice system to uncover new possibilities. In the United States, where much oriented research of this type—many would say too much—has been undertaken by contract between the defence services and the universities, very free conditions have prevailed.

For applied research fewer alternative paths exist than for most problems of pure research. Here the real problem is that of realizing a practical objective which brings its own satisfaction to the research worker. Many large industrial firms and government laboratories have found it useful, however, to allow a proportion of the applied research worker's time to be devoted to fundamental or oriented research of his own choice, to help to maintain his intellectual liveliness or to attract a limited number of first-class basic research workers to join the team, in order to bring new ideas and stimulus.

Government research laboratories in some countries, lacking the mobility of university research and with greater distance from the user of their work, appear to have difficulty in maintaining the level of creativity. Furthermore, problems exist concerning mission-oriented research laboratories which have partially succeeded in meeting their objective or the priority of whose work has diminished. It is very difficult to bring in new themes and missions to a laboratory of this type with a static population of men and skills. Furthermore, it is not easy, especially in a government structure, to stop work, liquidate a laboratory, and transfer its research workers elsewhere. Few countries have as yet solved this problem

The present atmosphere of impending change in the priorities of research with increasing need for multidisciplinary attack on a new range of problems suggests that attention should be devoted to new institutional approaches on the organization of research. One possibility of creating a more dynamic and flexible system would suggest that national institutions for research should be developed at three levels:

> *the strategic level*: where the over-all national problems and goals and the linkage between these goals and their research needs are discussed and general resource priorities determined;

> *the research planning level*: undertaken by a series of sectoral bodies, where scientists and users would determine broad programmes of research for each sector and, through expert panels, recommend where each project could best be carried out;

> *the implementation level*: where the individual programme elements would be undertaken within a wide variety of institutions, governmental, industrial, and academic, selected in terms of the appropriateness of the skills, equipment, and interests.

The OECD system of examination of national science policy

In situations of uncertainty and change such as exist with regard to science policy, countries are generally anxious to look at international experience and profit by the success and failure of the experiments of others. OECD created a special mechanism to meet this need through undertaking a series of explanations in depth of the science policies of its Member countries. A similar series of examinations is being carried out in the adjacent field of education policy. The procedure takes about a year in each case, and some three or four examinations in each of these fields have been undertaken each year. The first stage entails sending an OECD expert to the country under examination to prepare, after discussion with the various authorities involved, a background report describing the structure of scientific organization of the country, the statistics of its research expenditure and manpower, the background economic and social situation, and other related data. This preparatory work, which may take many months to complete in the case of countries such as the United States and Japan, is essentially descriptive and avoids value judgements as far as possible, although it may include formulations of the main issues facing policy-makers. The background report is submitted to the country and modifications relating to the accuracy of data or emphasis are sought.

In the next stage a group of high-level examiners, none of them nationals of the country under examination, having read the report, visit the country and question a broad range of individuals concerned. These may include the relevant ministers, senior officials, the heads of scientific institutions, university leaders, and industrialists. The people selected to undertake the examination are chosen after negotiations between OECD and the national authorities so as to provide a broad range of relevant experience. The team generally includes an economist. As an example of the type of individual chosen, we may cite the review of the United States, in which M. Théo Lefèvre (formerly Prime Minister and later Minister of Science of Belgium), M. Pierre Massé (former Chief Economic Planner of France), Professor Casimir (Scientific Vice-President of the Philips concern in the Netherlands), and Professor C. H. Waddington (Professor of Genetics at Edinburgh) constituted the team. The examiners' report analyses the main problem issues and frequently suggests points for consideration by the government in question or even proposals for reform. It is signed by the members of the team as individuals and is supplemented by a number of questions which they wish to pose.

The final phase is a so-called confrontation meeting held either at OECD in Paris or in the capital of the country concerned, during which the examiners question a team of representative science policy-makers from the country, often led by their science minister, in the presence of science policy-makers from the other countries who put further questions. Finally, a report is published which consists of the background report, the examiners' report, and a summary of the confrontation (*Reviews of national science policy: a series of individual country studies*, OECD, Paris).

This system has provided the Member countries of OECD with a detailed understanding of the science policy issues and experiments in the area as a whole. For the countries being examined the value has varied from case to case. At the outset the reports were somewhat descriptive and superficial, but as confidence in the approach grew, later examples have been much more profound and constructively critical. The effect has been important in the smaller countries, much less in the larger ones. In a number of cases major reforms have resulted, action being taken in some cases in the interval between delivery of the examiners' report and the confrontation.

Change and uncertainty with regard to national science policy arrangements persist. In April 1973, President Nixon announced the abolition of the President's Science Office and his Science Advisory Committee. Their functions have been transferred to an executive agency, the National Science Foundation (NSF), but with no extra funds or staff for the purpose. Dr. Guyford Stever, the energetic Director of NSF, will in future give advice on budget allocation for all civil science and on international science policy. He will report, not to the President, but to the Secretary of the Treasury. These moves clearly reflect American policy of a realistic attack on current problems of environment, health, transportation, crime, etc. and de-emphasize the research element.

The level of resources

7

A full analysis of scientific manpower and research expenditure is far beyond the scope of this volume, but it is necessary to give some indication of their order of magnitude in the different countries. The availability of statistics on these matters, which represent a significant fraction of national resources, is an obvious need, yet not much more than a decade ago, few countries had any quantitative measurements and, in fact, in many places governments and industrial firms were reluctant to provide data or at least to expose them to public and international scrutiny. The publication of the report to OECD by Freeman and Young (1965), comparing the situation in Europe, the United States, and the Soviet Union, marked the beginning of serious interest in resources for science and led to the long debate on the significance of disparities of R and D effort between countries on their economic and trade performance. Shortly after, the statistical and science policy experts came together to establish a common basis of procedure and method so that the data from different countries could be compared. The so-called Frascati Manual (1970), which records these agreements, has since been modified as the result of experience, and the original definitions, which covered only the natural and applied sciences, are being extended to include the social sciences. UNESCO has likewise broadened the scope of this work by extending its application to the less developed countries, while the matter is also regularly considered by the Conference of European Statisticians.

At the outset, it must be realized that a very high proportion of the research and development in the world is undertaken by the OECD countries and the Soviet Union. Some 86 per cent of the scientists and engineers of the world are concentrated in countries which have only 30 per cent of the world's population, while those engaged in research in the developed nations constitute about 94 per cent of the world's total. This situation is, in practice, still further aggravated by the fact that a high proportion of those active in research in the developing countries are engaged in fundamental research. As these countries are in the earlier stage of industrialization it is difficult to couple research and development with local industrial needs.

The great mass of world research is thus undertaken in the industrialized countries and particularly within the OECD membership. A series of International Statistical Years for research and development have been organized between these countries to permit comparisons of effort on the same time-base as well as in accordance with definitions and criteria commonly agreed. These statistics are, of course, always a few years in arrears, owing to the time required for gathering and analysing the data, first on a national and then on an international basis. Table 1 shows the evolution of research and development activities expressed as the percentage of that expenditure within the gross national product (GNP) of some twenty of the major research-producing nations. The last column expresses R and D expenditure in absolute terms.

A second measure of R and D effort is the manpower engaged in such activities. Table 2 gives the total numbers of qualified scientists and engineers engaged in research and development and also expressed in their numbers per 10 000 inhabitants of the countries in question. These figures are for the year 1969. The same table also gives the per capita GNP in each case as well as the per capita expenditure on R and D for the same year.

The gross national expenditure for research and development (GERD) for the United States amounted to $26 179 million in 1969, excluding capital expenditure by the Government. Other countries with high R and D expenditure were Germany ($3 044 million), France ($2 678 million), Japan ($2 592 million), and the United Kingdom ($2 440 million). The relative position of the United Kingdom has declined since 1964, when it came second after the United States. No other country exceeds a research expenditure of more than $700 million. These figures are, of course, at current exchange rates, which tend to underestimate the expenditure in some European countries and Japan. Equally, the figures are influenced by variation in the costs per research worker, which reflect not only general levels of remuneration in the various countries but also the level of sophistication (availability of expen-

TABLE 1

Gross national expenditure for R and D expressed as a percentage of GNP (at market prices)

	1957	1958	1959	1960	1961	1962	1963	1964	1965	1966	1967	1968	1969	1970	GERD 1969 (millions U.S. $)
Australia[1]							0·3				0·6		0·7		84·6
Belgium[2]							0·9		1·0		1·1		1·1		261·1
Canada[2]							1·1	1·2	1·3		1·4		1·4		979·2
Denmark	1·0	1·0	0·9	0·9	1·0	1·0					0·8			0·9	145·3 (70)
Finland											0·6		0·7		63·3
France[2]		1·0	1·1	1·2	1·3	1·4	1·5	1·8	2·0	2·0	2·2	2·1	1·9		2678·2
Germany[2,3]						1·2	1·4	1·5	1·7	1·8	1·9	1·9	2·0		3043·8
Greece								0·2			0·2		0·2		15·1
Ireland							0·4				0·5		0·6		22·4
Italy[2,4]							0·6				0·6		0·8		694·3
Japan							1·3	1·3		1·3	1·4	1·5	1·5	1·5	2592·3
Netherlands								1·9			2·2		2·1		585·5
Norway							0·7						1·0		
Portugal								0·3			0·2				
Spain[5]								0·2			0·2				97·0
Sweden											1·4		1·3		368·1
Switzerland								1·3			1·9		2·1		391·4
Turkey[6]								0·4					0·4		29·0
United Kingdom[2]		2·1			2·4			2·3		2·4	2·4	2·4			2439·8 (68)
United States[7]	2·2	2·4	2·6	2·7	2·8	2·8	2·9	3·0	2·9	2·9	2·9	2·9	2·8		26179·0

Source: OECD, 1972

(1) GERD 1969, taken from 1972 Federal Government Report.
(2) GERD data taken from national publications.
(3) GERD data include the social sciences.
(4) The 1969 GERD is not strictly comparable with those of the previous years owing to modifications in the method of survey used in the higher education sector.
(5) GERD 1964, Spanish pilot-team estimate, OECD Report, 1967.
(6) GERD approximate national estimates.
(7) R and D data include only current expenditure for the Government, private non-profit and higher education sectors; and current expenditure plus depreciation for the business enterprise.

TABLE 2
Per capita GNP and R and D expenditures: research manpower (1969)

Country	Per capita GNP at market prices (U.S. $)	Per capita GNP on R and D (U.S. $)	Qualified R and D scientists and engineers (number of full-time equivalents on R and D)	Qualified R and D scientists and engineers per 10 000 population
Austria	1730	11·5	—	—
Belgium	2380	27·1	6071	—
Canada	3250	53·9	21 040	10
Denmark	2870	29·7	3933	8
Finland	1970	13·7	2959	6
France	2790	53·2	54 692	11
Germany	2520	43·6	72 004	12
Greece	950	1·7	1042	1
Ireland	1190	7·7	1375	5
Italy	1530	12·8	22 723	4
Japan	1640	25·3	172 002	17
Netherlands	2190	45·5	10 954	9
Norway	2550	25·2	—	—
Sweden	3490	46·8	7537	9
Switzerland	3030	62·9	—	—
Turkey	370	0·8	—	—
United Kingdom	1980	43·8	—	—
United States	4660	131·3	536 000	26

Source: OECD

sive equipment, etc.) of the research effort.

Manpower comparisons have other technical uncertainties, but avoid the exchange-rate difficulty. In these terms, after the United States with 536 000 qualified research professionals, comes Japan with 172 002, while France (54 692) and Germany (72 004) have many fewer. However, since the size and population of the countries vary greatly, relative effort GERD as a percentage of GNP and qualified scientists per 10 000 of the population gives a better indication of comparative effort. The United States is seen to have a greater effort, not only in absolute terms, but in devoting substantially more of the GNP to research and development than the other countries, namely 2.8 per cent of the GNP and 26 qualified research people per 100 000 of the population. These tables show that the OECD countries fall into three clear groups as far as R and D resources are concerned. France, Germany, Japan, the United Kingdom, the United States, the Netherlands, Switzerland, and Sweden can be regarded as research-intensive countries; Belgium, Canada, and Norway are in the intermediate class; the rest are non-research intensive. It is surprising that one rather large industrialized country—Italy—falls into the latter category.

A main feature of these figures is the dominant position of R and D in the United States, both in absolute and comparative terms: considerably greater than the OECD European countries, Australia, Canada, and Japan together. A further interesting trend is the very strong growth of Japan during recent years, not only in terms of expenditure, but of available skilled manpower resources.

These are, of course, global figures. A more structured analysis would indicate, through the areas of concentrated effort of some countries in specific fields or industries, a more shaded picture. Data exist which reveal the distribution of national effort of the different countries, between direct expenditure of governments and those of industry and the universities; also for comparative efforts in defence, space, and nuclear R and D, as well as the balance between basic and applied research.

In view of the current interest in the utilization of sciences towards the solution of social problems and those of the tertiary sector, the figures in Table 3 are of some interest.

Table 3 shows the expenditure (by governments only) on research as a percentage of GNP for four major objective fields, using three separate years in each case. The expenditures for national security

TABLE 3

Estimated government R and D funding by major groups as
a percentage of GNP at market price

	National security and 'big science'			Economic development			Community services			Advancement of science		
	1961	1965	1969	1961	1965	1969	1961	1965	1969	1961	1965	1969
Belgium	–	0·13	0·17	–	0·12	0·17	–	(0·10)[2]	(0·16)[2]	–	0·14	0·21
Canada	0·22	0·24	0·23	0·19	0·28	0·43	0·02	0·06	0·11	0·09[1]	0·04[1]	0·09[1]
France	0·62	0·93	0·68	0·07	0·14	0·25	0·01	0·02	0·04	0·18	0·30	0·32
Germany	0·19	0·31	0·39	–	–	0·09	–	–	0·02	0·19	0·31	0·40
Italy	–	0·14	0·17	–	–	0·03	–	–	0·01	–	0·15	0·21
Japan	0·05	0·02	0·05	0·13	0·14	0·13	0·01	0·02	0·02	0·24[2]	0·31[2]	0·35[2]
Netherlands	0·09	0·16	0·19	0·11	0·15	0·22	0·07	0·08	0·11	0·26	0·41	0·46
Norway	0·09	0·12	0·10	0·12	0·19	0·22	0·04	0·04	0·05	0·18	0·24	0·29
Spain	0·03	0·04	0·06	0·02	0·09	0·11	–	–	–	–	0·03	0·03
Sweden	0·56	0·61	0·37	0·07	0·10	0·14	0·04	0·06	0·11	0·11	0·20	0·25
United Kingdom	1·10	0·92	0·69	0·14	0·16	0·32	0·02	0·03	0·05	0·09	0·14	0·17
United States	1·73	1·93	1·33	0·06	0·09	0·10	0·11	0·15	0·17	0·02[1]	0·03[1]	0·04[1]

(1) Advancement of research only.
(2) Probably overestimated compared with the other countries.

and 'big science' are extremely high for the United States, and high for France and the United Kingdom with considerable significance in the interpretation of the global situation of Tables 1 and 2. Thus Japan, which spends very little on military research, and Germany, which spends considerably less than the three countries mentioned, have therefore a considerably more intense effort for economic and other civil purposes than their position in the earlier Tables indicate. Government expenditure in direct support of economic development is relatively very high in Canada and high in France, the United Kingdom, and some of the smaller industrialized European countries. Research in support of community services— transportation, health, environment, urban problems, etc.—is in most cases an order of magnitude less than that for economic or defence purposes. Government support for research for the advancement of knowledge is relatively high in the Netherlands, Germany, Japan, France, and Norway.

Much has been said of late concerning the levelling-off of research resources. The data cited give some indication of this; for example, in the case of the United States. Understanding of these trends requires a more detailed analysis, however, which is now being undertaken. In the United States (and the United Kingdom) this has taken the form of less support for expensive technological development projects, especially in defence, nuclear energy, and space. Table 3, for example, indicates that the percentage of the GNP mainly devoted to defence research and development fell from 1.93 in 1965 to 1.33 in 1969.

8

Science and the economy

The relationship between science and the economy has been a theme of increasing interest during the past decade and has been discussed at each of the four ministerial meetings on science. Nevertheless, until recently the understanding of this linkage has been at a very naïve level. It has long been realized, of course, that fundamental discoveries in science have given rise to great new research-based industries. Modern power engineering would be unthinkable without a basic understanding of the laws of thermodynamics; the electrical and electronic industries were not even conceptually foreseen before the work of Faraday and his successors; the pharmaceutical and other branches of the chemical industry derive from the molecular architecture made possible by the development of organic chemistry. On the whole, economists have paid little attention until recently to the role of science and technology in economic and industrial growth: Keynes, for example, refers only marginally to technology. It was assumed that technology (and the research behind it) is stimulated and brought into being by the interaction of economic forces. There is, of course, much truth in this. In many instances, for example, inventions have been perfected mechanically before the level of labour costs made their use profitable. The scientist, on the other hand, saw the matter quite differently. His model depicted a basic discovery made in the laboratory by a pure research scientist motivated only by the urge to uncover new knowledge. Subsequently, and probably much later and in a distant country, an entrepreneur becomes aware of the possibilities inherent in the discovery, initiates applied research. If the matter appears to be economically as well as scientifically viable, technological development follows; a product or process appears on the market and fortunes are made, often with the original discoverer remaining in ignorance of the exploitation of his ideas.

This again is an oversimplified view but with elements of reality. We are coming more and more to regard technological innovation as a complicated process with scientific novelty being an initial input but far from the totality of the matter. Only a decade has elapsed since serious investigations began on the factors determining economic growth. The work of Schulz, Svennilson, Denison, and others opened the way to a better understanding of the place of technology. Denison (1962), in a study of the growth of the American economy since the beginning of the century, concluded that only some 40 per cent of the increase in the gross national product can be explained by additions to the traditional inputs of capital and labour. The greater part is ascribed to a residual factor, presumably consisting of a complex of elements, among which education, science, technology, entrepreneurship, and management skills have an important part. Essentially this study indicates that it is the quality of labour and the quality of capital utilization which have enabled the GNP to grow so rapidly. Manpower quality at all levels, from the unskilled worker to top management, is raised by education and training; capital utilization becomes more effective through technology, by the creation of new products, materials, and processes, by the markets they open up, and by increased productivity. While the validity of such work and its conclusions have been hotly contested, its broad lines have been generally accepted. Both education and science began to be regarded as national investments and as such found it easier to attract resources that hitherto. However, both governments and industries assumed, somewhat naïvely, that more research necessarily meant more growth. There was too little question as to the relevance of the research and to the coupling of its results within the innovation process. Nevertheless the right result was achieved, if for the wrong reason, in the building-up of the scientific infrastructure and resources in many countries where the research effort had hitherto been too modest. This was greatly encouraged by a new-found interest in research and development statistics, which as we have seen, were presented for the first time in a form which made international comparison possible. The league-table rivalry which resulted, with the United States at the top, acted as a spur to the other countries to increase their research expenditures.

At the second ministerial meeting on science, the disparity between the research capacities of different OECD countries, and particularly between that of the United States and those of the industrialized nations of Western Europe, raised questions about the significance which the R and D gap had for the economic performance and future trade patterns of the countries concerned.

The comprehensive studies by OECD of the technological gap, undertaken in consequence of this, formed the main theme of the third meeting of Science Ministers held in 1968. This meeting proved to be a turning-point in our understanding of the relationship between science and the economy—and much more. These investigations showed little direct correlation between a country's R and D effort and its economic growth or trade performance. It appeared that the diffusion of technology across frontiers, mainly in the form of purchase of patents and know-how or comprehensive arrangements between industrial firms, was sufficiently rapid to compensate for inadequacies in the domestic research effort or indigenous innovation. The example of Japan, with its highly successful industrial development based on imported technology, was a dramatic case in point. Studies of national balance of technological payments, however, proved extremely difficult in view of the inaccessibility of data.

It must be realized that effective transfer of technology can be relied on only for countries possessing a scientific and educational activity above a certain threshold. Such secondary or imported innovation, although it does not require such a high level of R and D effort as does the generation of new technology, nevertheless demands excellence in its educational systems and a sizeable spread of domestic research effort if the selection of relevant new developments from abroad are to be intelligently chosen and assimilated and if technological as well as managerial skills are to be available to put them to productive effect. Unless the level of national scientific awareness surmounts this threshold, a country can easily import the wrong patents, apply them ineffectually, and eventually innovate to obsolescence.

The OECD studies suggested, however, that a proportion of the technological innovation of a country aspiring to an advanced industrial position should be based on its own research and development if a real vitality were to be maintained. This is increasingly the situation of Japan, which, having built up its economic strength on imported technology, is now building up its R and D potential and cultivating original innovation. Thus the ratio of

Japanese receipts for technological exports to its payments for technological imports rose from 0.5 per cent in 1957 to 13.6 per cent in 1970.

The technological gap, demystified, thus proved to be inherently not a question of technology. Nor was it, as some suggested, a managerial gap. The basic process of technological innovation involves a complex series of elements, so that the assimilation of new knowledge from research cannot usefully be considered in isolation. Of the many factors involved, fiscal policy and availability of risk capital are important—as also are entrepreneurship, management skill and attitudes, labour relations, and marketing skill, as well as general levels of education and even national culture and psychology. It is only by understanding these individual variables and their interaction that the innovation process can be fully comprehended and mastered.

All the OECD countries, being committed to policies of economic growth, are concerned with stimulating innovation in industry. The policies adopted vary greatly. Japan considers the matter in terms of general industrial development policy; other countries encourage R and D through fiscal preferences. Canada has a system of direct subsidy to firms for research and development. In the United States, through massive programmes for defence, nuclear energy, and space, important government contracts for specific technological developments are accorded to industry while the government is the chief purchaser of highly sophisticated technological products. In the United Kingdom, support of the research associations, the nurturing of specific developments by the National Research Development Corporation, and direct subsidy of large industrial developments all have their part. OECD is at present analysing these various national measures to stimulate innovation with a view to correlating the experience, success and failure of the different approaches. In the meantime a study has been completed (OECD 1971) of the role of government in the innovation process. This analyses the problem from the point of view of industry, the research system, and the government. It stresses the importance of internal communications, discusses problems of the size and sophistication of markets, and looks at university—industry co-operation, as well as the influence of government procurement, taxation methods, standards, and many other aspects.

Conditions for successful innovation within the individual firms are closely analogous to those at the national level. The place of the research department and its linkage with company policy-making is fundamental. The research department is too easily isolated from general corporate policy and can, through the NIH ('Not Invented Here') complex, act as a barrier to the introduction of new innovations from outside. The firm, as the country, can expect to develop only a proportion of its new products and processes from its own domestic research, but to rely entirely on purchased technology can be dangerous unless, again as at the national level, the level of scientific awareness, based on its own research capacity, is high enough to allow a quality scanning of the world possibilities. It seems that the management of innovation generally depends on entrepreneurial quality outside the research department, and that the coupling of research and marketing is particularly important. A study by Professor Freeman and his colleagues at the University of Sussex, the so-called SAPPHO Project (1972), is particularly significant in this connection. A series of pairs of innovations—failures alongside parallel successes—were analysed. Clear-cut differences within the pairs fell into a consistent pattern. Successful innovations were seen to have a much better understanding of user needs, to give considerable attention to marketing (particularly to a forward education of the market), and to make more effective use of outside technology and scientific advance.

Science as a system: the place of fundamental research

9

For many years there has been controversy on the place of science in society, the extent to which it can be planned, and its own internal needs for the maintenance of high levels of quality and creativity (Brooks 1968). The subject is greatly confused by the inclusion of both science and technology within the concept of science policy, two systems which, as we have seen, although inextricably inter-related have quite different structures and imperatives. Most of the arguments refer essentially to fundamental research, pursued for its own sake and hence often regarded as a consumption item, a cultural expenditure which can well be afforded and is highly desir-able, as are corresponding activities in the arts and humanities, by all vital cultures. However, it is increasingly obvious that the interface between fundamental and applied research is becoming ever more diffuse. Furthermore, a very large proportion of funda-mental research undertaken in the industrialized countries is oriented towards application in that it seeks to extend the frontiers of knowledge in areas of interest for technological or social develop-ment. Such research, justified by its promise for application, how-ever indirect this may be, is dominantly financed by government and industry and is hence part of the joint system science–technology. Even pure researches, conducted without any sense of a possible 'usefulness', are inescapably part of this same system, in addition to being cultural goods, in that they may profoundly influence the quality and vitality of the total system as well as its direction in the long term.

The Marxist view that science is completely determined by economic and social needs has polarized the opposite view in the free economy world that science is an autonomous system which must be granted complete freedom if it is to have a maximum quality and benefit. There is here an implicit assumption, similar to that of *laissez-faire* economics, that maximum scientific growth as maximum economic growth will tend to maximize all other desirable social goals—a contention which is more and more questioned. There is, nevertheless, a basic need to allow a high degree of freedom to pure research and, indeed, to much fundamental oriented research if it is to maintain a high level of creativity, but this argument is all too easily made by scientists who claim such freedom as an inalienable right. This might well be admitted in relation to the relatively few research leaders of creative genius but difficult to accord to the growing mass of scientific workers whose contributions are much more pedestrian.

Growing suspicion that unrelated growth of technology and economy may be diminishing many aspects of the quality of life necessitates a fresh look at the place of science. At the 1971 meeting of science ministers of OECD countries, there was indeed unanimous agreement that science could no longer be regarded as an autonomous system producing knowledge for its own sake although incidentally, if importantly, making all sorts of applications possible through the separate process of technological development. The focus of attention is now on the articulation of science policy on the whole range of national sectoral policies to which it can or should contribute. In this view, science is to be considered as an important sub-system within the total national system, thus emphasizing the concept of national development *through* science. The question at once arises as to whether a viable science policy can arise in the absence of, or in insufficient contact with, equally coherent policies and strategies; for example for education, health, urban affairs, or economic and social development in general. Government responsibilities have became so extended and deal with problems so complex that they cannot be tackled by traditional administrative methods, and they badly require new knowledge from research if policy and decision-making are to become effective. On the other hand, contemporary science and technology are too pervasive of national policy as a whole to be left in the hands of the specialist experimental scientists. The economist by himself, the sociologist, the administrator, or the politician is likewise impotent to solve most of the problems of the world today.

The relationship between science and the various bands of the broad spectrum of public affairs is perhaps most clearly illustrated in terms of interacting systems. The total national activity or system is conveniently, although in a necessarily somewhat arbitrary manner, divided into a number of sub-systems such as those of defence, education, industry, agriculture, health, social welfare, foreign policy, etc., for each of which exists some degree of deliberate policy associated with national goals, more or less clearly defined. In the past, for purposes of administrative convenience, the creation of these sectoral policies and the conduct of operations concerning them has been undertaken more or less independently. In reality, however, each of these activities overlaps to a greater or lesser extent with the others, although the interfaces and zones of overlap are not too clearly delineated. In fact, the machinery of government, designed for operation in a less complicated world of slow change, implicitly assumes that these sub-systems are virtually autonomous, although it allows for some co-ordination of their respective activities by means of not too effective interdepartmental committees. The zones of overlap and indeed the mutual interaction of the policies which govern them are frequently not recognized overtly by the government machine, which makes it difficult to solve problems and administer services in these no-man's lands—or rather two, three, four, or more men's lands.

The scientific effort of a country can be represented by one such sub-system, which overlaps all the other sub-systems in a three-dimensional model. There is, indeed, at the centre of the science sub-system an area which does not cover any other national sub-system, although it possesses an important and diffuse interface with the education sub-system. This is the area of fundamental research, which is the reproductive mechanism of the science sub-system and essential for the maintenance and constant regeneration of the whole. This is one area for which a science policy in the simpler sense of 'policy for science' should be possible, at least in theory, although even in this zone the proportion of the total resources available is governed not only by finance availability but by diffusion across the interface from education (research manpower), and its optimum size may depend on factors other than the maximum good of science itself. There are, of course, many feedback mechanisms from the various zones of overlap in the system as a whole. The areas of intersection with other sub-systems such as health or agriculture cannot be governed by policies determined by science alone, but represent penetrations of new knowledge and of scientific method *per se* into the total fabric of society and, conversely, of practical experience and evolving problems of society into the consciousness of science.

Fundamental research is thus seen as an activity supported by society as an adjunct to the education system and important for its vitality at the higher levels, as a method of apprenticeship for the production of research manpower, as the chief means of adding to human knowledge, and as one of the main cultural activities of our times. The construction of the huge particle accelerators, such as those at Brookhaven and Geneva, the objective of which is to enhance our knowledge of the basic structure of matter, has been seen by some as the building of monuments to man's intellectual striving, in their significance not unlike the medieval cathedrals. Clearly then, the basic policy problem in the choice, resource allocation, and implementation of such investigations is how to achieve the highest possible quality, even if national prestige may be the obvious motive for their financing. This is attempted in all countries through the advice of outstanding scientists in the various specialist fields. This intimate involvement of the scientific community in resource allocation for fundamental science means that the strong forces of the internal sociology and ecology of science tend to determine the relative allocation and to influence its magnitude. The mechanisms of allocation, through research councils and their panels, departmental grants, and contract devices, etc. in a sense tend to elucidate what the natural distribution of promise and fashion between the various disciplines and sub-disciplines is at the time. The system of judgement by peers inevitably reflects internal scientific criteria. Mission-oriented agencies using this system endeavour to elaborate criteria of relevance to their missions, but in practice these are applied by the candidate for a contract or grant, especially in the United States, by his selection of the agency or sub-agency to which he applies and by the selecting panel on the basis of their own knowledge of the different qualities of various research schools and individual workers. Scientific merit is, of course, one of the chief criteria, but there is a tendency to accept the already successful and scientifically respectable: 'To him who hath shall be given'. Many other criteria may, however, intervene. In the United States, for example, where the concentration of the research effort in the great universities of the east and of the west coasts is politically difficult, a regional bias may be introduced to help build up high-quality facilities in the middle. Such equalization policies may lead initially to a diminution of research efficiency in the narrow sense, but may in the longer term be justified by the stimulus towards a wider distribution of the best in higher education and of quicker diffusion of science and technology.

On the national level, discussion of expenditures on fundamental research governed by these complex considerations is very difficult, and the absolute level is seldom determined deliberately. Each nation tends to accord to technology and applied research what it considers appropriate and what can be afforded. Beyond this it supports fundamental research as a sort of fixed overhead. In practice, although this is seldom a conscious process, this overhead represents a striving for that threshold of scientific awareness necessary for rapid and effective innovation in technology and society. It is the total effort which counts—or should count—irrespective of the size of a country, rather than the proportion of its G.N.P. devoted to fundamental research. One might expect that smaller, advanced countries, which have a need for intimate knowledge and skill over the whole spectrum of science, if their technology and innovation are to be soundly based, should decide to devote a larger proportion of their resources to fundamental research than the larger countries, which can more easily achieve the threshold. This is, however, not the case. Price (1966), in a study of the output of scientific papers country by country, has shown that each nation contributes to the literature in about the same proportion as its GNP.

The changing nature of science

In the meantime, science itself is undergoing a profound transformation. The complexity of the problems of contemporary society demands ever more the contribution of many disciplines working together. There is therefore an increasing need for multidisciplinary teams. The concept of multidisciplinarity is very fashionable, but although much lip-service is paid to it, symbiotic working between the disciplines is difficult and exists only to a minor extent. Integrative leadership for such work is rare and university and research structures, static in their conception, are so far unable to generate it. There is great need for fresh thinking in education and research with a view to providing more flexible structures and enhanced possibilities of mobility. Without this, problems will receive but fractional and unbalanced attention.

Within the natural sciences themselves, a new and more dynamic approach appears necessary. In the universities and elsewhere, science is still being taught and practised in terms of the classification of disciplines devised in the middle of the last century and which long appeared to be so neat: little boxes marked chemistry, physics, geology, botany, etc. As the content of these subjects filled up, interface subjects such as chemical physics and biochemistry began to appear and later more complicated intersections, such as molecular biology and cybernetics. Less clearly defined fields of growth have also been emerging, such as the study of brain and behaviour, which lies at the point of convergence of a number of disciplines including molecular biology, neurophysiology, biochemistry, and psychiatry (see OECD Report 1972). Such subjects are, in fact, not permanent disciplines or new categories of science but foci of advance, temporary scientific fields, which can be consolidated only by multidisciplinary approaches. They will later extend by merger with other approaches from equally transient points of knowledge to create new and probably equally temporary outposts at the frontiers of understanding, within which the forces of science will assemble for still further penetration into the unknown.

This may well be the general trend of scientific development in the future: not individual static sciences growing linearly but a dynamic interaction of various lines of approach from different disciplines within the total fabric of knowledge, advancing where and when promising opening-points appear or where complex problems lead. Inevitably such a concept must encompass the social sciences and eventually also the humanities. Such a dynamic model of the scientific system cannot readily evolve within our present institutional structures. The organization of both education and research will require basic reform if the flexibility is to be provided without which the existing sciences, stretched to the point of diminishing return, will insufficiently penetrate and interact with the evolving totality of human knowledge.

10
International co-operation in research

Like all intellectual activity, science is inherently international. The results of fundamental research are published freely *in extenso*, abstracted, and available in all parts of the world, thus adding to the corpus of human knowledge. Through attendance at meetings and seminars organized by innumerable international bodies for specific scientific disciplines and sub-disciplines, by visits to laboratories of foreign colleagues, through visiting professorships, the opportunities offered by sabbatical years, exchange fellowships, correspondence, etc., individual scientists have constituted a truly international scientific community, sharing interests, attitudes, and values which often transcend cultural and ideological barriers. Research differs, however, from many other forms of intellectual activity in that its practice in many instances involves joint experimentation or shared programmes on an international scale.

Technology, on the other hand, since it involves property rights, is more restrictive in its contacts, although through the patent system, firm-to-firm exchanges of know-how, and the purchase of processes, the diffusion of technology across national boundaries is remarkably quick. The proprietary nature of technology and the fact that much fundamental research is application-oriented throws some shadow of competition on to the process of international research co-operation, which is enhanced by national rivalries and the prestige engendered by research success. International scientific activity is thus a subtle blend of co-operation and competition.

There are four main motives for undertaking research on an international scale.

(1) Many fields, such as astronomy, oceanography, meteorology, some aspects of environmental research, tropical diseases, etc. cannot be restricted within the confines of a single country, and

from the early days of experimental science these were the fields in which international co-operative programmes developed.

(2) The fields of 'big science', such as high-energy physics, space, some aspects of nuclear research and astronomy, demand exceedingly costly equipment, often beyond the means of all but the largest countries. The only way open to smaller countries to retain a significant knowledge of and activity in such research is through international co-operative schemes which, by means of cost sharing, provide the necessary facilities. In some of these subjects, the next generation of equipment may be so costly that scientific advance will be possible only through co-operation schemes on a world scale.

(3) In many subjects, particularly newer fields such as molecular biology, where there are, as yet, few specialists in each country, progress can be achieved by the intellectual cross-fertilization which international projects can provide. This can, however, be achieved through providing means to facilitate the mobility of scientists by common programming, etc. and not necessarily by the creation of international institutions when especially expensive equipment is not involved;

(4) A number of fields of applied research, particularly within the public domain, are only marginally competitive and, as problems are common to many countries, organization on a nation-by-nation basis involves a high degree of duplication. There is a strong argument, therefore, for the establishment of programmes either internationally developed or in common to adjacent countries in a region. An example is road research.

A very large number of international scientific organizations have arisen in response to such needs. Some of these, such as the international scientific unions, are independent organizations of scientists themselves, often subsidized by national or international (e.g. UNESCO) funds. Others are intergovernmental bodies, among which those that have arisen in Europe since the Second World War are the most prominent. The proliferation of such organizations and their propensity for growth, as well as doubts as to their efficiency, is of great concern to their member countries. Such organizations have mainly been established on the basis of scientific enthusiasm or—as some would say—pressure or in response to immediate political needs. They have arisen one by one on an *ad hoc* basis and without any over-all policy on international scientific needs. It is not possible in this short book to describe or analyse the functioning of these organizations. The following remarks will, therefore, be restricted to consideration of some of the policy issues and particularly to the need for a more organic linking of national and international resources for research.

The essential need is perhaps for countries to regard their international research commitments more deliberately in terms of the national science policies. Contribution to international schemes are, in the end, justified if they provide an extension to domestic research resources or if they enrich these or remove a proportion of unnecessary duplication. If this is to be a dominant criterion in deciding whether a country will or will not adhere to a particular international research scheme, it will be essential for the country to possess an internal mechanism for discussion of international research co-operation and its function of complementing work within the country. Yet in extreme cases the finance for an international project may come through a government department different from, and with little contact with, the department responsible for financing domestic effort in the same field. In many instances also, there is no real co-ordination of policies towards the different international organizations. Frequently responsibility for representation of a country on the steering organs of a certain international organization, and hence responsibility for briefing of delegates, will be in the hands of a particular department or sub-department. The national delegates naturally tend, over a period, to evolve a loyalty to the international organization in question. The national attitude expressed towards the particular international organization may well be incompatible with that of representatives of the same country at another international organization, with resulting confusion. It might be argued that a more realistic solution would be found in a rationalization of the international organizations with a clear delineation of the field of activity of each, so as to avoid overlap. This cannot, however, be achieved in present circumstances. The different national membership of each, from the nine of the Common Market, the eighteen of the Council of Europe, the different NATO grouping, the twenty-three of OECD, to the complete world coverage of UNESCO, means that exclusive attention to a particular scientific subject by one of these bodies would exclude from participation those countries which were not members.

There is, therefore, need in each government for a point where its internal and external science policies can be related; where national attitudes and briefs towards the whole range of international scientific organizations can be harmonized, participation decided, and the views of all national agencies concerned with different facets of research brought together. Such a group would be in frequent touch with similar centres in neighbouring countries for exchange of views and planning of future international work. Without such mechanisms in each country and the co-ordination of domestic and research effort which it would make possible, decisions on international science will remain a series of *ad hoc*, little-related, and at times contradictory decisions.

Difficult problems arise with regard to growth proposals from existing international research bodies, especially for the smaller countries. When such organizations are set up initially, the scales of national contribution are generally established on a basis of population, GNP, *per capita* income, or some combination of these. The proportion of the budget paid by a small country may therefore be quite modest, yet as the international budget grows, although the proportion to be contributed by the small country remains small, its absolute value can easily rise to a level greater than national support to the same subject domestically. Some means will have to be found to provide a more flexible scale of contributions if such countries are to retain a balance of effort between national and international activity in particular fields.

When proposals to create new international science organizations are put forward, frequently by groups of experts meeting as individuals rather than as national representatives, it is difficult for countries to decide on membership or to judge between several alternative schemes. What happens on many occasions is that the protagonists of one of such schemes persuade a government to call a preparatory conference, and when this is done it is usually this particular scheme, subject to some modification, which eventually finds support. It would seem preferable to provide a forum in some existing international organization to allow for various proposals to be discussed informally and countries to be given time and opportunity to discuss with their neighbours the merits of each before they are faced with a decision one way or the other. At the second meeting of OECD Science Ministers, it was suggested that three criteria should be applied in such cases.

(1) The project should be well supported by the national experts in the field, not merely as a proposal considered in isolation, but in response to the question as to whether it is the best way of using such resources as may be available.

(2) The purpose of the project should be to undertake desirable scientific work which cannot be undertaken effectively on a national basis, either because it is beyond the resources of the country concerned, because there is a lack of sufficient specialized manpower, because the research must be carried out over a wide geographical area, or for some other concrete reason.

(3) There should be a solid basis of national interest in carrying out the project, judged in relation to the participants' own national science policies. At times scientists in a particular field, dissatisfied with their own national situation or even that of individual universities, may seek remedy by promotion of an international scheme. In fact, the state of affairs they wish to remedy may derive from defects in their national science policies or financing mechanisms.

Many problems exist concerning the structure and management of international research enterprises. If science is to flourish, bureaucratic control must be kept to a minimum. But this is difficult with a dozen or more countries involved, each with different administrative and political objectives regarding the institutions. One of the most important results of international co-operative work is a maximization of effort with each participatory country providing through its outstanding workers elements of special skills which add up to a totality which is qualitatively superior to that which the individual countries could master. Often, however, in intergovernmental organizations the enterprise is regarded too easily as a mere consumer of national resources and the principle of *le juste retour* applied, whereby each country expects to receive back, through the salaries of its nationals in the scheme, contracts for equipment and buildings etc., the same proportion of resources as it contributes. This may be financially sound, but it can make nonsense scientifically, since it ignores the value of the intellectual contributions of a country which may be paying only a modest financial proportion.

This type of difficulty argues strongly for the exploration of new and more flexible types of international research structure and management. Where especially expensive equipment is involved, there is undoubtedly a need for central installations for the sharing of costs, despite the management problems which they involve. The generally recognized success of the European Council for Nuclear Research (CERN) at Geneva indicates that these difficulties can be overcome by wise scientific direction and restraint on the side of the officials. The success of CERN, however, encourages adoption of its pattern where the arguments for centralization within a single institution are much less justified. There seems to be a need, therefore, to explore the possibilities of a wider range of institutional alternatives for international science. In many fields, particularly that of fundamental research, the greater need is not for agreed centralized projects, but for arrangements to encourage the cross-fertilization of ideas, ignoring national frontiers. In some cases, the most effective measure may well be the simple provision of funds, under the control of the scientists themselves, to allow for easy and frequent communication, more frequent periods of work in foreign laboratories, etc. In other instances, however, there is a need for the establishment of common programmes, related to the particular research being done by the countries or institutions concerned. Having identified unnecessary duplications and gaps in the approach, such common programming would then be followed by agreement to share the tasks on a voluntary basis between interested laboratories, to exchange research workers, and to use the results in common. By such means it should be possible through bilateral, regional, continental, or world co-operation to undertake substantial programmes of research without the provision of central international funds with all the political negotiation and control which this implies.

This type of 'uninstitutionalized' international co-operation is particularly promising for fields of applied research which, in most countries, are the direct responsibility of governments and contain only minor elements of competitive rivalry; subjects such as building research, food investigations, hydraulics and other public works, road and other safety problems, research on standards, earthquake protection, exploitation of geothermal energy, environmental and pollution research, and the testing of possibly toxic materials which come into the environment or are used as drugs or food additives. As examples of this type of research OECD has already gained considerable experience in this direction by the establishment of a programme on road research (that is, road construction, road and automobile safety, and traffic control), which has already given rise to a number of important co-operative research projects voluntarily undertaken by groups of interested countries and without the establishment of an international research fund. In this scheme a small international secretariat of only five professional staff has been assembled with two functions. The first is the establishment and operation of a first-class computerized information system, which probably saves the participatory countries more than the cost of the central secretariat. Secondly, a series of 'state of the art' studies of particular aspects of the problem area are made which, by comparison of the various national programmes, give rise to international research projects and often form the basis for regulations and harmonized national policy decisions. Such a scheme could easily be extended to transportation research in general.

Finally, there is a need to establish some type of international forum for the discussion, without commitment, of proposed new schemes of international research, for the review of success and failure in existing approaches, the study of methods of co-operation appropriate in specific cases, and for the establishment of common criteria.

Science and the developing countries

This subject requires deep analysis with a view to reform of the policies and practices in the donor countries, and with regard to the problems of science and development. This is beyond the scope of this book, but since it is an essential part of international research activity, some aspects must be mentioned briefly.

It has already been stressed that science policies have been considered too much in isolation from their social and political context. This is tragically true with regard to the potential of science and technology for the benefit of the less developed countries. The industrialized nations possess over 90 per cent of the world's scientific workers, yet three-quarters of the world's inhabitants live outside this favoured area. Furthermore much of the research undertaken within the 'third world' is in the interest of the industrialized countries and much of the rest is economically sterile and often irrelevant. If, then, science is to contribute to economic and social development on a world scale, its use in solving the problems of development is a major challenge.

Many of the problems of application of research to the needs of the developing countries relate to obstacles within these countries and are in fact themselves aspects of underdevelopment. We have already noted that, in such countries, the ratio of fundamental to applied science is abnormally high. This is because such countries do not have the means to assimilate technology. Most of the research workers in developing countries have been trained in the laboratories of the industrialized nations and on return home have found little use for their skills in the solution of local problems. They tend, therefore, to try to continue lines of research begun during their foreign visits in universities which are all too often inappropriate copies of academic models of European or American institutions and then become, as it were, expatriates of the international scientific community working under great difficulty, and all too easily becoming part of the brain drain back to the advanced countries.

The transfer of technology from industrialized to backward countries is often unsatisfactory. The recipient countries often lack the institutional knowledge and capital necessary for the efficient use of western technology, which has been developed in the direction of high capital intensity. Furthermore, modern techniques are often applied to small industrial sectors in the poor countries, without being adapted to their total situation or without taking account of the local manpower and educational situation. In addition, they have to operate within a market where rules are largely set by the advanced countries and in accordance with their interests.

It is therefore necessary to think of the effect of science and technology and of the donors in three senses: first, so as to help the developing countries to build up institutions and activities oriented directly towards the most urgent economic and social problems; secondly, to advise on the creation of mechanism and policies which will allow foreign technologies to be imported and adapted so as to suit local needs and traditions; thirdly, to devote a more substantial part of their own research programmes to the solution of technical problems that the developing countries are not yet in a position to tackle themselves.

In most of the OECD countries, science aid falls outside the function of the science policy mechanism and is the responsibility of development agencies, for which it is of somewhat marginal importance. The scientific community is, on the whole, more aware of the potentialities of science for development than are the government authorities and would welcome a more important proportion of the national science resources being devoted to such activities. It is important that development science should be progressively brought within the scope of general science policy. This was a major recommendation of the Brooks Report (*loc. cit.*) which went on to suggest that the industrialized countries should formulate research programmes in favour of the developing countries in their own laboratories, and that they should pool their resources with a view to more effective attack on the problems of development and the making known of the existence of knowledge relevant to the needs of the developing countries. A start has been made by OECD in compiling an inventory of research in progress in the member countries of importance to problems of development and there is also an enquiry on work in progress and the need for new research in a number of fields selected as of particularly high priority by the United Nations Advisory Committee on the Application of Science and Technology to development problems.

This is, however, only one aspect of the problem. It is only by the creation in the developing countries themselves of new technical institutions that research and development can be evolved to respond to the real economic and social needs. The building of a network of research and development institutions in the 'third world' will necessitate a much greater and more systematic effort in the industrialized countries to provide a flow of scientists and engineers who will spend limited periods of time in the developing countries. Such work may well become a normal stage in the career of many scientists of the OECD countries, and will not only contribute to the solution of problems of the development and life in the tropics, but also contribute greatly to the understanding of the real nature of these problems in the donor countries.

Science and society

11

Economic growth—end or means?

The rapid growth in the national resources devoted to research and development during the past decades has been paralleled by an equally sharp rise in the gross national product of the industrialized countries of the world. This would seem—at least superficially—to endorse the economic growth justification for increasing science budgets of the period, despite our still imperfect knowledge of the relation between science, technology, and the economy.

The OECD countries, which comprise the industrialized nations of the market economy world (Western Europe, North America, Japan, Australia and New Zealand), are responsible for about three-quarters of the world's commerce and for about the same proportion of research and development undertaken in the world. In 1969 the ministers of the countries of this economic region set a target of 50 per cent increase of the GNP of the area, taken as a whole, for the decade of the 1960s. In the event, this target was surpassed and would have been greatly so if Japan, which joined the Organization during that period, had been included at the outset. Prospects for the same countries for the 1970s are no less ambitious. OECD forecasts that 'provided adequate policies are followed, this trend should go on gathering momentum over the coming decade and should allow a 60–70 per cent growth of GNP in real terms for the membership as a whole'. In other words, the average real income *per capita* of the population would more than double by 1980 as compared with that of 1960. This is a degree of wealth with no parallel in history or in any other part of the globe.

One might have expected that at this point, where the most important group of industrialized and trading countries had attained a threshold of affluence, these results would have been greeted as a triumph. On the contrary, they were considered with sober caution, without drama, and indeed with a caveat: growth yes, but what is it for? What about quality of life?

On 23 May 1970 the OECD Council, meeting at ministerial level, issued a communiqué containing the following paragraph:

> Ministers stressed that growth is not an end in itself, but rather an instrument for creating better conditions of life. Increased attention must be given to the qualitative aspects of growth and to the formulation of policies with respect to the broad economic and social choices involved in the allocation of growing resources.

This statement does not appear to have been given the attention it deserves. It marks the end of the era of growth for growth's sake and the beginning, however faltering, of a new approach to growth as the provider of resources for the broad needs of society.

The acceptance of growth as a major national objective has led to a number of contradictions. On the one hand, it has given rise to inflationary pressures, generated in all segments of society, which are likely to increase and become a major economic issue of our times as each organized group competes for a larger share in a growing GNP. Much of this inflationary pressure arises in the lagging areas of the public sector with low productivity and little research and development. As standards of living increase, the gap between the actual situation of the individual and his expectations widens, especially at the lower end of the scale. This is equally true as regards rich and poor countries since expectations have become internationalized thanks to the media. What is sometimes called 'the persuasion industry' has created artificial demands throughout the population for what are essentially the requirements of middle-income groups in the rich countries, replacing to some extent the effects of public works programmes of the past. The luxuries of the last decade become the necessities of the present, with vast changes in life-styles, including the automobile society (with the accompanying deterioration in public transport) and the television culture among other disadvantages. Again, many items which were formerly supplied through the market mechanism have become public goods, such as universal education, health care, welfare services, housing, recreational facilities, and so on.

On the other hand, faith in economic growth is evaporating in the minds of many, in the face of unease and suspicion about its prospects for the quality of life, the increasing difficulty in managing the growing complexity of economic and social systems, and the appearance of unwanted and unforeseen side-effects of technology and growth. For technology is all too easily seen as the cause of these ills and behind technology a science which can place men on the moon but which seems impotent to improve the human condition. It is not only the policies, priorities, and resource demands of science which are in question, for its public image has been shattered and its mystique exorcized. Many people—and especially the young—are obsessed by the negative manifestations of science through the bomb, the menace of chemical and biological warfare, fear of manipulation, destruction of the environment, deterioration of the quality of urban life, and loss of satisfaction in work.

Problems of contemporary society: the problematique

The objective of national affluence, formerly accepted without question, is thus showing its ugly face with symptoms of social disorder, violence, university troubles, the alienation of individuals, and the monstrosity of urban life. Governments are, of course, concerned with the new range of problems which seem to face all successful industrial societies and there is a deep need to reassess the place of science and technology in a society which has at the some time ever-widening expectations of material acquisition, which exerts increasing social demand for education, health care, better cities and services, and which also denounces the adverse by-products of the technology that has helped to provide its affluence.

It may be useful to enumerate those problems in more detail. At the economic level, they include inflation—ever more difficult to control—balance of payments difficulties, recurring monetary crises, and unemployment. Then there are the problems of environmental deterioration, not only in the immediate and visible matters of gross pollution of air and water, but also in relation to the accumulation in earth and oceans of non-biodegradable toxic compounds, the building-up of carbon dioxide in the atmosphere, thermal pollution, etc., most of which could be controlled by technological and economic measures well within our means if we had the will to do so. However, we know far too little about the long-term effects of our actions on the environment and do not sufficiently understand the systems with which we are dealing to steer sensibly between hysteria and complacency and to institute control measures based on rational tolerance levels. Much basic research is required here, as also with regard to the possible long-term carcinogenic, genetic and other effects of the innumerable chemicals which we ingest in the form of pharmaceutical products, food additives, cosmetics, etc.

The urban environment generates another cluster of problems: the cluttering of cities with automobiles, deterioration of public transport, the removal of solid waste, suburban sprawl with its cultural deserts, and in general the increasing frustration and discomfort of city life with its commuter agonies and the growing 'lemming syndrome' of irritation and selfishness which the juxtaposition of too many people seems to engender. There is also the more general problem of automobile safety with a mounting level of road accidents with high economic as well as human costs—a phenomenon which is somehow tolerated in silence, in contrast to public indignation and hysteria with regard to relatively minor dangers.

A further group of problems surrounds the educational system which, with its long life-cycle and the slow effect of reform, produces in the young an image of irrelevance. The system appears to many as preparing young people for a style of life and employment which is evaporating before their eyes and is being replaced by a drab world of uncertainty in which they will live and work. With a large proportion of the 18–24 age-group in the universities, many of whom lack a clear vocational direction, it is not surprising that their somewhat artificial, quasi-adolescent status within essentially traditional and academic institutions should lead to unrest and political exploitation.

These and other difficulties seem to be producing a degree of social disequilibrium—high rates of crime, delinquency, and drugtaking. Large number of people just do not see the point of working for a living but are often passively critical parasites on a system which they reject. This rejection and, more broadly, questioning of the values of our contemporary, materialist society is accompanied also by a resistance to control and planning and a general sense of individual frustration and isolation.

Finally, there are the major problems of poverty and underdevelopment. In industrialized societies, these are dramatically manifested as ghetto and racial difficulties, but the main danger for the future may well be in the poverty gap between the industrialized nations and the over-populated third world.

This array of problems of scale and rapid change gives a special character to the difficulties facing contemporary society. Their variety and universal character gives rise to much discussion as to their immediate cause. Many of them are apparently products and even biological consequences of affluence, arising when the pressures of poverty and survival no longer seem too pressing—when the state is generally regarded as all-providing and at the same time cold, distant, and immovable. A second cause is to be found in population increase and particularly the concentration of its major proportion in cities—often associated with high industrial density, pollution, and overcrowding—where, with greater leisure, more sophisticated but not always wise amenities arise. Finally, there is technology with its dehumanization of work which, through its contribution to productivity, empties the countryside, fills the cities, and provides the affluence. Technology is the all-too-obvious scapegoat and science shares the blame as its progenitor.

These problems, generally seen individually, have a number of features in common. They seem to appear in all countries, or in social groups within countries, which have surmounted a certain level of economic development, irrespective of the political or social system. They are, by nature, extremely multivariant and have elements of an economic, social, psychological, political, and technological character. Furthermore, they seem to interact with each other in ways which are only dimly understood.

There is a tendency to refer to this cluster of problems as 'the *problematique*'—a series of difficulties so intermeshed that it is increasingly difficult to identify discrete problems and apply discrete solutions. To tackle the elements of the *problematique* one by one appears increasingly as a vain attempt to remove the symptoms of a disease which has not been fully diagnosed, with the consequence that interactions within the system may lead to further difficulties in other parts which are not obviously recognized as being due to the initial remedial action. Such circumstances have, of course, always existed. They have become obvious now as a result of a greatly increased scale and tempo as well as through the inescapable inter-dependence of countries as a result of technological development and modern communications. Aspirations can no longer be restricted within the village or the nation: with radio and television they have become universal.

The concept of the *problematique* throws into question many of our institutional and policy arrangements. Government departments, universities and research structures all reflect a vertical type of sectoral structure appropriate for the regulation of individual difficulties, but difficult to apply in relation to the horizontal interconnections of today's problems.

Technology on trial

Growing preoccupation with the *problematique* has, as we have seen, given rise to increasing public suspicion concerning technology and has thrown a shadow on scientific research, on which technological development ultimately depends.

One manifestation of this is a growing opposition of individuals and communities to the creation of new power stations (especially those operating on nuclear fuel), oil refineries, and similar installation in some countries, despite the fact that the same individuals and communities eagerly demand their products and resent brown-outs. Amongst the young there is a feeling that technology is an ugly manifestation of a greedy, unthinking, and uncontrolled capitalism, although in fact the same symptoms are appearing in socialist states. As a consequence, it is difficult in some countries to attract students to the natural sciences and engineering, in contrast to the flow towards sociology and other behavioural subjects, in spite of promising career prospects. Research in subjects such as molecular biology is regarded as potentially evil because of the power of manipulation of man's brain and thoughts to which it might ultimately give rise.

Yet in reality it is unwarranted to blame the contemporary difficulties on technology or even the existing priorities in research and development. These effects are consequences, not of technology as such but of man's unwise use and management of it and of too short-sighted social and economic policies. It is largely irrelevant to put technology on trial. Ever since the invention of fire, the plough, the lever, and the wheel, technology has been man's main means of groping his way upward from poverty and disease. It is hardly more sensible to blame technology for the modern ills than it is to condemn the hand that holds the assassin's knife. The real fault lies in the need, motivation, and society of men who wield the knife and who misuse technology. Today each one of us has at his command many times the mechanical force of the frail human body, but there is little sign that human wisdom to manage and control the force has deepened during the last 2000 years. The problem therefore is essentially that of the wise management of technology, which is part of the socio-economic system and which can hardly be controlled or redirected except as part of that system.

The fourth meeting of Ministers of Science of the OECD countries

The fourth meeting took place in October 1971 and had as its general background the Brooks Report, *Science, growth and society*. This was the first meeting of ministers to reassess the role of research and development in the context of the growing social problems. They agreed that public opinion was focusing too much on the negative effects of science and technology, rather than on the benefits the public enjoyed as a result of scientific discovery. On the whole, the balance has been strongly on the positive side, especially through the contributions of research to economic well being which gives the possibility of abolishing poverty in the industrialized countries and of reducing the disparity between rich and poor among the nations. Success in prolonging life and conquering disease was equally impressive. Nevertheless, there was real reason for concern over the unwanted side-effects of technology, and too little use had been made of science in solving social problems. There was need for more rather than less research, but a considerable degree of reorientation was required if the increasingly complicated problems of modern societies were to be solved.

The meeting agreed that science could no longer be regarded as an autonomous area of policy; in future it would have to be developed more closely in relation to formulated national objectives and, in particular, intimately co-ordinated with economic, social, and education policies. Nearly all the problem areas now facing industrialized societies can hardly be attacked by the economist, the engineer, the natural scientist, the behavioural scientist, or the politician separately. These problems all have economic, social, and political facets and hence new multidisciplinary attacks would have to be mounted. This would eventually require considerable change in both the research and the educational systems.

With regard to the main trends of research and of science policy for the next decade, the ministers foresaw three major thrusts. First, their governments were all committed to policies for the stimulation of further economic growth, and this in turn would mean further technological development and the scientific research to sustain it—that is, more science in the traditional and, at present, contested sense. This would call for a greater understanding of the process of technological innovation, the development of improved methods for the formulation of policies for science and technology, and the establishment of research priorities and better means of decision-making.

However, it was unanimously accepted that the new technology would have to be socially acceptable. The second thrust of science policy should, therefore, be concerned with the management and control of technology. In particular, it was necessary to develop and apply methods of technology assessment and to evaluate, not only the economic but also the social and even cultural consequences of various technological options. Not only is it necessary to prepare in advance to ensure that new 'hardware' processes do not provide unpleasant surprises in relation, for example, to pollution effects or worker opposition, but that whole fields of development, such as the use of the computer in education, should be thoroughly investigated in relation to probable effects on the individual student, the training and methods of teachers, and the evolution of the educational system.

Technology assessment is a difficult and imprecise subject. Little exists, as yet, in the way of an established methodology. As the Japanese expressed it at the ministerial meeting, we can only learn by doing. A number of approaches for assessing the social and economic consequences of specific technological developments or fields are being planned in various countries, and it is expected that their results will be compared internationally so that experience can spread rapidly and, it is hoped, some relatively reliable techniques of assessment will evolve. Meanwhile, OECD is compiling a 'state of the art' study in this difficult new field to serve as a basis for national developments, methodological and otherwise.

It should be realized that technology assessment is only one element in the difficult problem of the management of technology—a subject which raises difficult political and ideological issues. If governments, through social pressures, are to take seriously the need to ensure that future technological development is acceptable to the workers and to the public at large, many difficult decisions will be required and conflict areas will appear. For instance, with the need for more technology to assist in achieving economic growth, accepted by all the OECD governments, their policies must aim at stimulating technological innovation and at providing a suitable climate for it by fiscal and other means. At the same time they may have to inhibit or modify specific developments on social criteria. These are issues difficult to resolve. Equally, industry, whether in the private or the public sector, may fail to solve the problem of reconciling their role as institutions of society with their individual profit-making motivations.

The third direction for future research priority identified by the ministers was the use of science and technology in solving the problems of the social and service sectors under direct government sponsorship. Many of the current problems of society arise from inadequate development of technology in the service (or tertiary) sector, in comparison with that in manufacturing industry and agriculture. The social and service sectors represent a very large and increasing proportion of national investment, but in general their productivity, mainly unmeasured and difficult to measure, is probably low and their management is somewhat amateur and untrained in comparison with that of industry. It is to be suspected that the very slow growth of productivity in government services and in the service sectors generally, particularly in education, health care, public administration, and urban affairs, has been a major cause of inadequate social performance of the economic system in relation to individual and social welfare.

Furthermore, the research and development inputs into these sectors are marginal. Preliminary statistical analyses indicate that the research and development resources in such fields, calculated as a ratio of the importance of these sectors to the total economy, is more than an order of magnitude inferior to that for industry or agriculture. Innovation in sectors such as education and health is very slow and unsystematic. The forces of the market do not provide incentives for change such as those that operate in industry. If we know insufficiently the nature of the technology innovation process, we know next to nothing about innovation in the service sectors.

In some of these fields, and particularly in transportation, the development of 'hardware' technology is now proceeding rapidly, although a great deal of extra effort is required. Again, the computer is an important technological element in all service sectors. There is in addition, however, a need to look at the service sectors from a systems point of view, to apply the scientific method through operational research and other techniques, to develop 'software' technologies, and to encourage a more comprehensive use of the scientific method in decision-making. All of this will entail the cultivation of the social sciences in multidisciplinary relationship with engineering and other aproaches.

The communiqué of the ministerial meeting noted the need for 'expansion of research, development and innovation activities to meet social needs such as environmental quality, health, education and urban development'. In particular it recommended that OECD should extend its work to innovation in the service sectors of the economy and study the contributions of science and technology in these fields and on the work environment. The ministers also invited OECD to prepare an intergovernmental conference on the social sciences to identify priority research tasks.

This meeting marked an important point of inflection in the evolution of science policy. The ministers whose countries are the main producers of research and development unanimously agreed that scientific development must in the future evolve in co-operation with social and economic policies, that an increasing proportion of research and development resources must be devoted to the problem of society, and that multidisciplinary development of research is essential. This would have been unthinkable even five years ago. The response of their programmes to this agreement will inevitably be slow and will invoke many difficulties. The meeting coincided with what may only be a temporary levelling-off of the growth of R and D resources in the United States and some other countries. This slowing-down is caused mainly by policy changes affecting large projects in defence, space, and nuclear energy. The newer fields, such as the environment, are in the growth phase, but are starting from a very low base-line. The main problem now faced for the first time by science policy is one of adaptation and change of programmes and priority skills. In many countries large government laboratories have become partly obsolescent, their mission partly accomplished or their priorities lowered. It is not easy to use space engineers on environmental problems or social research, and hence there may well be a period of hiatus with a degree of unemployment of technicians. Equally, there is need to reconsider mechanisms for research programming and implementation to provide a more flexible system which can respond to change.

Postscript
Science policy: the new perspectives

We have seen that in the short span of the last fifteen years science policy has emerged as an accepted element of national concern, with its own, if uncertain, place in the machinery of government. It has evolved quickly, modified and extended its concepts but, alas, retained most of its initial problems. With the recent understanding that science policy must increasingly be considered in intimate relationship with other areas of policy, the question arises as to whether it will persist as a discrete subject or be merged into the complex of long-term policy and planning. Are, in fact, science ministers still necessary?

The answer can be given only tentatively and through a separate look at the two faces of science policy: policies for science and science for policy.

It is more necessary than ever to have clear policies for the management of science as a significant element of national expenditure and activity: the optimum use of resources, the preservation of creativity. Problems of resource allocation, establishment of priorities, centralized versus sectoral approaches, and extension of national resources by international cooperation are still unresolved. Still more important is the need to evolve the science system in a more dynamic form so as to respond to changing needs and new types of problems; institutional changes such as those suggested on p. 59 will have to be considered. The growing need to develop multidisciplinary approaches to the new problems is again a further task which will add greatly to the already growing problems of university reform and educational relevance. The development of the social sciences to a level of maturity from which they can make real contributions to policy-making is critical. These and other new challenges will necessitate greater attention being paid to policies for science, which must continue to have a political focus in each government, under a minister, however his portfolio may be named.

Science for policy raises quite other issues and requires quite different modes of approach. As the Brooks Report (1968) states,

science is in disarray, because society itself is in disarray, partly for the very reason that the power of modern science has enabled society to reach goals which were formerly only vague aspirations, but whose achievement has revealed their shallowness and created expectations which outrun even the possibilities of modern technology.

Understanding of the subtle and complex relationship between science and society is at a very primitive level; it is intimately linked to the value-system of society, which is at present seriously challenged, partly as a consequence of the very success of technology, but without much probability of early consensus on an alternative.

For the immediate future it would seem that there are three separate aspects of this relationship which warrant attention.

(1) How can research in the natural, social, engineering, and human sciences help in solving specific problems of social importance, within the context of the *problematique*?

(2) How can science help in the formation of national goals and in clarifying their underlying values?

(3) How can research contribute to a better understanding of policy problems, the relationship between policies, understanding of the nature and interactions of the *problematique*, improvement of the decision-making process, and the development of more appropriate institutional structures?

It is not possible here to pursue these themes in detail. The first has been discussed in the previous chapter. The second depends on the establishment of a relationship of mutual confidence between the decision-makers and their science advisers, so that the latter are fully aware of policy difficulties and the former soberly informed as to the potentialities of new knowledge for the solutions of their problems. Inter-goal conflicts must also be seen and delineated, since the implementation of policies towards the achievement of a particular national objective will often have an important impact, positive or negative, on efforts to achieve quite other goals. Thus technology aimed at encouraging economic growth may, by its unwanted side-effects on the environment, reduce the quality of life; the spin-off from defence research may in the opposite sense have useful technical and managerial benefits in economic sectors. The reciprocal influence of research achievement and the value-system is a still more dangerous nettle to grasp. New technologies require new markets. These are at present all too often conjured up by the 'persuasion industry', irrespective of their long- or short-term social desirability, with further generation of consumption and probable waste, leading to further consolidation of our old material values and, by polarization, of hostility towards the society which tolerates and encourages them. Indeed the whole concept of an indefinite continuation of economic growth in its present form is in question. The real problem is perhaps not growth as such but to determine, on a value basis, the desirable quality and structure of that growth for the continuing general good. The scientific research of the future as well as the 'software technology' derived from it will therefore have to aim not only to achieve sectoral or single-goal innovation but to foresee its broad consequences on the whole series of objectives of society.

The third of these themes was raised by the recent meeting of science ministers, which stressed 'the need for research into the policy-making process itself'. Many governments are becoming aware of the inadequacy of their structures and policies when faced with the complexity and interlacing of the contemporary problems. Such structures, designed for earlier, simpler times, are generally in the form of vertical hierarchies, without the complement of an adequate staff structure such as large industrial corporations or military organizations have found so necessary. The linkage of sectoral programmes, research or otherwise, and their co-ordination within a government's over-all policy is generally the task of the cabinet or the prime minister, although vestiges of a staff structure are often to be found in cabinet secretariats or 'senior departments'. In many instances the real integration may in fact be achieved by the finance minister, with the result that balance and co-ordination is achieved through the budgetary mechanism rather than on deeper policy considerations. Interdepartmental co-ordinating committees (for example, on research) in most countries develop into vested-interest groups, each representative defending his own preoccupations and by tacit agreement respecting those of the others. Incremental changes may be discussed if the mass of on-going work is seldom challenged. The considerable extension of government responsibility of recent years, as well as the obviously horizontal nature of the activities involved, has made this problem acute. In urban affairs, environment, transportation, and, not least, science, responsibility falls fractionally within the functions of a whole array of vertical departments of mission-oriented agencies. This has forced governments to experiment with various mixes of departmental responsibility through, for example, the creation of super-ministries or ministers. Such solutions do not appear, however, to work out too well, with the consequence that in some countries there has been continual change in recent years. Science and technology are particularly telling cases of this uncertainty.

Another approach now in fashion is the creation of various types of 'think-tank' or centres for the study of alternative policies and strategies. The recent creation in Canada of a number of 'horizontal' or staff ministers and of a Scientific Council on the Problems of Government in the Netherlands likewise aim at structural innovation and improved policy-making.

A second feature of the situation is the power and often inertia of the bureaucracy. No matter how intelligent and objective its members may be, nor how well-intentioned its corporate spirit, civil servants are selected to provide stability and continuity as political governments come and go, and hence they find difficult the tasks of innovation and management of change. This is particularly so in countries such as Britain, where a change of government leads to the injection of only a small number of political personalities per department who, overwhelmed by the variety and mass of detail which confronts them, do not find it easy to introduce change against the momentum of on-going activity and tradition.

In many countries, and especially those such as France which possess highly centralized government systems, there is a rising demand for decentralization and wider participation in decision-making. To many the ideal of a participative democracy is appealing, both for the establishment of social goals and for assuring that science responds to them. Yet the more groups and interests which participate, the more are their goals and ideals likely to conflict with a consequent increase in difficulty in reaching clear decisions. At the same time, as we have seen, the growing complexity of problems necessitates a higher degree of consideration of their mutual impact and makes difficult participative decision on a problem-by-problem basis. Thus participation and the need for harmonization are difficult to reconcile, and here again bureaucracy is the traditional means of achieving consistency. Only in one country associated with OECD, namely Yugoslavia, is there a policy of broad participation in reaching decisions, combined with a high degree of decentralization. Each of the constituent republics and regions of that country possesses a 'science community', an association responsible for science programming and the distribution of research grants by broadly based participation. It is much too early to forecast whether such a system, which can easily sacrifice economic efficiency and programme coherence to obtain participative management and enthusiastic identification of its scientists in their work, can prove successful. Clearly there is need for much deep thinking and experiment on these difficult problems.

A further dilemma faces governments with regard to their policies —science and otherwise—in decisions regarding the balance between long- and short-term problems to be tackled. The cycle of some four years between elections is a feature of parliamentary democracies and has the consequence that both government and opposition parties have to respond to the immediate issues which concern the electorate. Governments, like individuals, tend to ignore longer-term problems which can be put off until tomorrow. Until recently, this probably did not matter too much, since the long term was indeed far off and could be coped with as it gradually approached. Today, however, with increased scale, complexity, and quick public perception of change, social, economic, and technological as well as political, what could formerly be regarded as of long-term importance seems to race into the period of five to ten years ahead. As a result, we are tending to fall into a rhythm of crisis management staggering from one emergency to another—. monetary, social, balance of payments, inflation, unemployment, and the rest—adopting remedial measures but seldom tackling the fundamental issues.

Furthermore, the growing interdependence of nations makes it well-nigh impossible for single countries, however serious their efforts may be, to solve such problems in isolation. Foresight is particularly necessary in science policy and for the effective use of technological capacity. The 'development gap' between a new concept in the mind of a scientist and the first appearance of its results, as a product on the market or as a social innovation, may take upwards of ten years. In circumstances of rapid change such as those of today, concentration of effort on the solution of the immediate and obvious problems can too easily mean that the solutions appear too late, that science and technology are concerned with the solution of yesterday's problems. This applies mainly to major discoveries and innovations and there is, of course, constant need for technological improvement which comes through a continuous application of known scientific and technological principles, through better use of materials, new control methods, improved processes, and so on. The ministers of science stressed the need to develop our scientific capacity in intimate linkage with economic, social, and other policies, but since these policies are themselves in rapid transformation, the science policy of today should ideally be articulated with the social and economic policies a decade hence. This is clearly impossible, but the argument for regarding science policy in a prospective sense is extremely strong. There is much talk, especially in the United States, of a forthcoming energy crisis, especially with regard to petroleum products. Much is hoped for in the development of nuclear power: fast breeder reactors in the relatively near future, and perhaps fusion energy eventually. Yet there has been until recently little evidence of phased planning of new energy sources in response to future needs, taking into account the importance of petroleum as a chemical raw material and possibly also as a basic source of protein for a hungry world of after 1985—to say nothing of the need to take into account social, environmental, and political aspects of the power problem. Work on better methods of production and use of other fossil fuels is still less obviously geared to long-term demand for energy.

The consideration listed above would seem to indicate that one of the new and immediate tasks arising from the science for policy concept is the development of the new field of policy research. Already a large number of dispersed efforts are being made to develop knowledge relevant to policy-making. These include new approaches and multidisciplinary studies, often combining elements of operational research, systems analysis, cybernetics, information theory, strategic analysis, futures studies, systems engineering, theory of games, decision theory, and similar fields, with important inputs also from more traditional fields such as economics, political science, and psychology. As yet, however, this field of research is not clearly delineated, its methodologies are tentative, and work is very fragmentary and dispersed. Policy science seeks to deal with the contributions of systematic knowledge and structural rationality to the design and operation of social and political systems by integrating knowledge from many disciplines. It is conceived as an aid to, and certainly not as a substitute for, the policy decision-maker by providing objective data on alternative decisions.

Another aspect of this problem relates to the elucidation of the complex of interacting problems which we have termed the *problematique*. The nature and extent of the interactions between the various elements within the cluster of difficulties confronting contemporary society is largely unknown, but it is extremely important that they should be understood. Sponsored by an independent group of scientists, humanists, and industrialists, known as the Club of Rome, an important although imperfect first study has been made of the interactions between some of the more important quantifiable variables of the world situation, such as population and economic levels, food requirements, agricultural possibilities, pollution, and depletion of raw materials, and these have been projected to the future. This has been done using the systems dynamics technique of Professor Jay Forrester (1971) of the Massachusetts Institute of Technology. It does not aim to provide a forecast of the future situation, but is rather a cross-impact study of present trends, indicating what might happen unless policy and other changes intervene first, in order that this be done intentionally rather than as a result of crisis and disaster. In a sense it is an example of what might be called 'propylactic futurology'. This highly controversial pioneer study has already had considerable political impact but is essentially important in having stimulated both its supporters and detractors into undertaking a whole series of new research projects using different assumptions and methods. At least twenty such researches are at present in progress, some of them under direct sponsorship of the Club of Rome, which is, incidentally, conceived as a non-organization—a catalyst without political ideology, ambitions, or bureaucracy.

Science for policy, therefore, while so intimately linked with the problems of managing national and world scientific effort as such, has many features which lie well outside the traditional fields of scientific research and which are extremely complex and difficult. Whether responsibility for such approaches will fall within the portfolio of Science Ministers is difficult to say. More probably, the need for deeper insight into the relationship between science, economic, social, educational, and other policies, taking a longer view of national and world trends than has hitherto been thought necessary, will become an essential responsibility of governments and will be attached to central planning offices or those of the prime ministers. Science policy in this new sense will extend far beyond the definitions with which we began. It will be regarded perhaps as policy for the mastery of technical and social progress or, more widely still, as policy for the generation of new knowledge required by man to increase his understanding of himself, the universe, and his societies as well as the penetration of such knowledge in the management and evolution of society. This is too broad a task for a single minister of science.

References

BROOKS, D. H. (1971). *Science, growth, and society—a new perspective.* OECD, Paris.
—— (1968). Can science be planned? In *Problems of science policy.* OECD, Paris.
BUSH, V. (1945). *Science, the endless frontier*: A report to the President on a programme for post-war scientific research, United States Government Printing Office, Washington. Reissued by the National Science Foundation, July 1960.
COUNCIL OF EUROPE REPORT (1972). *On the results of the third parliamentary and scientific conference.*
DENISON, E. F. (1962). *The sources of economic growth in the United States and the alternatives.* Report before U.S. Committee for Economic Development, New York.
FORRESTER, J. W. (1971). *World dynamics.* Wright Allen Press Inc., Cambridge, Mass.
FRASCATI MANUAL (1970). *The measurement of scientific and technical activities: proposed standard practice for surveys of research and experimental development.* OECD, Paris.
FREEMAN, C. and YOUNG, A. (1965). *The research and development effort in Western Europe, North America and the Soviet Union.* OECD, Paris.
MEADOWS, D. *et al.* (1972). *The limits to growth.* Earth Island Publications, London.
OECD REPORT (1963). *International scientific organisations*—catalogue preceded by introduction on some aspects of international scientific co-operation. OECD, Paris; *see also* (1962). *International Scientific Organisations Grants to Their Libraries and Information Services.* Library of Congress, Washington.
—— (1965). *Ministers talk about science.* OECD, Paris.
—— (1971). *The conditions for success in technological innovation.* OECD, Paris.
—— (1972). *Problems and prospects of fundamental research in multidisciplinary fields—brain and behaviour.* OECD, Paris.
PIGANIOL, P. (1961). *Science and the policy of governments; the implication of science and technology for national and international affairs.* OECD, Paris.

References

PRICE, D. J. DE SOLLA (1966). The science of scientists, *Medical Opinion Review*, No. 10, 88–97.

SAPPHO PROJECT (1972). *Success and failure in industrial innovation.* A summary of project SAPPHO. Centre for the Study of Industrial Innovation, London.

SPAEY, J. (1969). *Development through science.* UNESCO.

WILGRESS, D. (1960). *Co-operation in scientific and technical research.* OECD, Paris.

Further reading

BEN DAVID, D. J. (1968). *Fundamental research and the universities.* OECD, Paris.

CALDER, N. (1969). *Technopolis.* Macgibbon and Kee, London.

DUPRE, A. H. (1961). *Science in the Federal Government.* Belknop Press of Harvard University Press, Cambridge, Mass.

FREEMAN, C. (1969, National science policy. *Phys. Bull.,* **20**.

GABOR, D. (1964). *Inventing the future.* Penguin Books, London.

—— (1972). *The mature society.* Secker and Warburg, London.

JONES, G. (1971). *The role of science and technology in developing countries.* Oxford University Press.

KAPLAN, N. (ed.) (1965). *Science and society.* Rand, McNally, Chicago.

KING, A. (1964). Science and technology in the new Europe. *Daedalus* **95**, 434.

—— (1968). *Science and Education in OECD—an experiment in international cooperation.* In a report issued by U.S. Congressional Panel on Science and Technology, Washington DC.

—— (1971). Science Policy, changing concepts. In *The place of value in a world of facts* (Nobel Symposium). Almqvist and Wiksell, Stockholm.

MEADOWS, D. *et al.* (1972). *The limits to growth.* Potomac Associates, Washington DC and Earth Island Publications, London.

OECD REPORT (1971). *Science, growth and society* (the Brooks Report). OECD, Paris.

—— (1971). *The conditions for success in technology innovation.* OECD, Paris.

—— (1965). *Fundamental research and the policies of governments.* OECD, Paris.

—— (1965). *The social sciences and the policies of governments.* OECD, Paris.

—— (1972). *The research system, Vol. I, France, Germany and the United Kingdom.* OECD, Paris.

ORLANS, H. (Ed.) (1968). *Science policy and the university.* The Brookings Institute, Washington, DC.

PIGANIOL, P. and VILCOURT, R. (1965). *Pour une politique scientifique.* Nouvelle Bibliothèque Scientifique, Flammarion, Paris.

Further reading

PRICE, D. K. (1964). *Government and science, the dynamic relationship in American democracy.* New York University Press.
—— (1965). *The scientific estate.* Harvard University Press, Cambridge, Mass.
PRICE, D. J. DE SOLLA (1963). *Little science, big science.* Columbia University Press, New York.
ROSE, H. and ROSE, S. (1969). *Science and society.* Allen Lane, the Penguin Press, London.
SALOMON, J. J. (1970). *Science et politique.* Editions du Seuil, Paris.
SNOW, C. P. (Lord) (1961). *Science and government.* Harvard University Press, Cambridge, Mass.
SPAEY, J. *et al.* (1969). *Development through science.* UNESCO, Paris.
WIESNER, J. B. (1965). *Where science and politics meet.* McGraw-Hill, New York.

Index

Index